Writing

WORKING IN THE THEATRE

**AMERICAN
THEATRE
WING**
Founder of the Tony Awards®

EDITED BY
Robert Emmet Long

FOREWORD BY
Paula Vogel

A GINIGER BOOK

continuum

NEW YORK • LONDON

2008

The Continuum International Publishing Group Inc
80 Maiden Lane, New York NY 10038

The Continuum International Publishing Group Ltd
The Tower Building, 11 York Road, London SE1 7NX

The K. S. Giniger Company Inc
250 West 57 Street, New York NY 10107

www.continuumbooks.com

The Tony Awards are a registered service mark of the American Theatre Wing.

g green press INITIATIVE Printed in the United States of America on 30% postconsumer waste recycled paper.

Library of Congress Cataloging-in-Publication Data

Writing : working in the theatre / edited by Robert Emmet Long.
foreword by Paula Vogel
        p.   cm.— (Working in the theatre)
    "A Giniger book."
    Includes index.
    ISBN-13: 978-0-8264-1806-7 (hardcover : alk. paper)
    ISBN-10: 0-8264-1806-6 (hardcover : alk. paper)
    ISBN-13: 978-0-8264-1807-4 (pbk. : alk. paper)
    ISBN-10: 0-8264-1807-4 (pbk. : alk. paper)   1. Dramatists,
American—20th century—Quotations.   2. Playwriting.   3.
Drama—Technique.   I. Long, Robert Emmet.   II. Title.   III. Series.
PS352.W75   2007
808.2'41—dc22

                                                    2007028687

Contents

Foreword by Paula Vogel

When I came home from my first semester in college to the subbasement apartment I had shared with my mother, I made my announcement: "I'm going to be in the theatre." My mother staggered to the sofa, sat down, and started to weep. Almost as if a death in the family had been announced, instead of my future, Mother sat shivah on that sofa for a week.

To be fair, I was the first generation in the family that had graduated high school and the first generation to go to college. We knew no one in theatre, nor did we know any artists in any field. We knew government workers, secretaries, postmen, salesmen, all reliable, steady workers who paid their rent on time, and dreamt their dreams on two-week vacations until retirement. Theatre in my neighborhood was aligned with dinner theatre, or mystery theatre trains or cruises you might take on an anniversary. The epitome of artistic success among my mother's colleagues would be to appear someday on *Hollywood Squares*.

"Your mind!" she wept. "You could go to Law School!"

Little could we guess that my mind has never had a dull day in the course of pursuing playwriting as a profession. With the skills of diplomats, the strategy of lawyers, the pitching skills of sales executives, and the organizational skills of marketers, playwrights use both sides of the brain. I often think of playwriting as a form of three-dimensional chess: If I write this line, how might the actor counter? The director? How do I create emotional space on the page without dictating choices to a designer I have not yet met? What moves do I make in strategies that make the responses fun, challenging, and open to multiple possibilities for my collaborators, some of whom may not yet be born?

I imagine that the readers of this volume might buy this book to support their own choices of a present and future dedicated to playwriting, and this book will give you a very different reception than the one my relatives gave me. There are lovely snippets to savor from our colleagues in the field, and which will hopefully renew our own calling.

Each year I give a seminar to younger writers that I call "The Biz Seminar," and the principles take the same amount of time as it would take to drink two bottles of wine with a friend during a late-night chat (we also sometimes refer to the seminar as the "Two Bottles of Wine" talk). I must be brief in these pages, but here are some of the basics we discuss as we pass the bottle.

It's not a matter of being good at parties, schmoozing, or knowing and dropping names. It is a matter of being truthful; when you discover peers or artists in whose work you believe you must find ways to tell them about the gifts they've given you. Find a small handful of colleagues that you would work with for free, for sweat equity, for the thrill of working with them, and that becomes your circle. All you need are five artists to build a theatre; ten to build a movement. In the field of art, circles rise together, faster than any individual artist can.

Discard the notion that artistic survival is based on a Darwinian struggle for survival that goes to the fittest. Survival can be based on sharing aesthetics, finding a home in a circle, supporting the artists around you, and challenging yourself by being thrilled by the work of others. If you are thrilled, and write from that sense of joy, you will respond on the page with an energy that we can never find from comparison and envy.

The Laws of Supply and Demand are a terrible model for the arts. The more good or great art exists, the more we develop a taste and demand for great art. The more great artists surround me, the better my chances that I will become better at my art. Supply in the arts can create demand.

Most of all, the greatest gift we can give as artists is generosity: Generosity to other artists, generosity to younger artists, and generosity in terms of our own shortcomings. There's always another rewrite; another new play to write in between the rewrites; a chance to go back and rediscover your script years later. Most likely, we've all heard a constant refrain from relatives, teachers, friends, strangers, who give us practical advice on how to spend our lives: Not in the arts! There is, from preschool, a tendency to suppress the artistic drive in favor of more pragmatic skills. And so we are all practiced at self-censorship in this society. It is easy to edit or procrastinate, and very hard to expose a first draft to a room of strangers and friends. We must be supportive to ourselves as well. So here is the basic summation of my "Two Bottles of Wine" seminar.

If you don't write your experience, the life you imagine, the life you witness, no one else will. And I won't get the experience of witnessing that life from my seat in the theatre. That desire to walk in others' shoes is one of the most compelling desires I know; if you write it, others may be able to re-imagine their own lives from the world you've created.

Life is long enough for two or three careers. It may be that you are struggling to meet deadlines as a younger writer as you juggle two or three jobs; it may be that you juggle child care or family care with stolen moments, or that you are facing a blank page after decades in other fields. What is the worst that can happen? That you find fellow travelers who love theatre as much as you do; that you can afford a modest bottle of wine for a late-night (or depending on your age, an all-night) discussion about theatre. In ten years' time, you will have spent that time and conversation with colleagues who have become some of the great artists in the field, and that wine that you shared will be, in your memory, more delightful than money itself can afford to buy (whether money earned from the law, investment banking, marketing—any gainful employment that pays well and is urged upon you by friends and family). If, however, law or banking is your passion, and writing an enjoyment on the side, I still urge you to write: We need those plays, too.

I hope you follow your passion. I hope you write. I hope to read your thoughts in a book the American Theatre Wing publishes in the future. I hope I see your play in the theatre.

Introduction

This book on writing for the theatre grew out of the enthusiastic response of viewers to the American Theatre Wing programs on the profession of theatre today. The series is called
Working in the Theatre for good reason. The participants
have devoted their lives to the theatre and can speak about
this experience as insiders.

Most of the participants included in this volume, the
third in Continuum's *Working in the Theatre* series, are re-
nowned dramatists. Others are young contenders who have
been giving new directions to the theatre. This compilation
is not primarily intended as a guidebook in creative writing
or as a "practical guide" for aspiring playwrights. More a
mosaic, this is a book to inform and inspire readers regarding the many dimensions of working as a successful playwright today.

One aspect of this book that is apt to strike the reader is
its diversity, as many of the best-known playwrights of our

time have their say. Perhaps their most important insights involve the role of the solitary author, who is the first to put his or her ideas on paper, in a collaborative enterprise. Indeed, the art of the playwright predates history: self-expression through storytelling represents a universal human aspiration and activity. But likewise since the beginning of recorded time, without those with the means to produce, without the actors, without sufficient direction to bring these elements together, the playwright does not have a platform or stage for theatrical self-expression.

One of the most compelling aspects of the book is the way the speakers draw the reader into the theatrical life, with its frustrations and triumphs, dead ends and inspirations, all in the name of collaboration. The collaboration of writer and director, writer and actor, writer and dramaturg, writer and producer, applies to dramatic theatre but even more so, in many ways, to musical theatre. Novelists and poets work alone, and their lives necessarily involve them in solitude. The playwright is acquainted with loneliness too. But he or she also experiences rehearsals, rewrites, opening-night jitters, and the ecstasy of seeing a personal vision performed in real time before an audience.

It is, therefore, part of the theatrical experience that the playwright should work as a member of a team. Many relevant issues are raised in the course of these conversations. How does the writer relate to his or her audience? When are workshops useful and when not? Do the actors influence the staging of the play? How do writer and director interact? What about the writer who directs his or her own play? Is the dramaturg helpful to the playwright or a hindrance? How might the theatrical venue affect the writing? These questions, which in some ways have no clear or single answers, are deftly probed.

A final word is in order regarding the structure of this volume and the process of turning fleeting conversation into the permanence of a book. It has been organized to bring together recurring themes from more than thirty years of transcripts in the *Working in the Theatre Seminars,* and in so doing to create a rhythmic and dynamic work consisting of as many voices as possible. Comparable, contrasting, or divergent views are arranged for maximum effect. Synthesizing many thousands of pages of conversation, literally from different eras, into one modest-sized volume, to showcase the range of the American Theatre Wing programs as well as what it means to be a playwright today, has been challenging. Some of the excerpts have been lightly edited to provide fluency in the conversations. Basic biographical sketches and an index are included for easy reference.

ROBERT EMMET LONG

1

Starting Out

Bill Russell

In sixth grade, the teacher went around the room and asked us what we intended to be when we grew up. And I said, "A playwright." And everyone turned around and asked, "What's that?"

Arthur Kopit

It's not as if you're saying, *Well now, I think maybe I should go to medical school. Should I go to law school? Should I become a playwright?*

David Henry Hwang

I was born and grew up in L.A., so I was home for the summer, between my junior and senior years. I saw an ad in the *L.A. Times* Calendar: STUDY PLAYWRITING WITH SAM SHEPARD. So I thought, *That's good,* and I clipped it and sent it in. This turned out to be the first year of the Padua Hills Playwrights Festival, which since then became fairly well known. But because it was the first year, there were only two of us who applied—and we both got in.

David Auburn

I didn't know I wanted to be a writer. In college, I wrote a play. On a whim, I submitted it to this fellowship program that Universal Studios ran. I went out to Universal after I finished school and I wrote two screenplays. I still had no idea what I was doing. I had sort of stumbled into it, and the fellowship ended. I was sitting there in L.A., with these two screenplays that no one wanted to make into movies, and I just really didn't know what to do. But I had a pretty clear feeling that if I was going to go broke, I would rather go broke trying to be a playwright in New York than trying to be a screenwriter in L.A.

Adam Rapp

I used to draw a lot when I was a kid. And I think, for fiction writing, I was tapping into something that was very visual for me. I think theatre is another expression of that—where there's something in a frame that's happening. There's a story three-dimensionally passing through space and time.

Lanford Wilson

I was the absolute best artist in Ozark High School—Ozark, Missouri. In fact, I thought that I was the new Gauguin. I was going to be a painter. At the same time, I was also very interested in theatre. I went to San Diego State, and suddenly there were about forty artists who were better than I was. So, I started concentrating on writing. But I was writing short stories.

For some reason, I didn't know that plays were written: they came in those little books, and I didn't know anyone ever wrote them, except Samuel French.

I got a job working in an advertising agency in the art department, and it was so boring that I started writing on the tracing paper in the notepad. I wrote a bunch of stories, and I have a collection of rejection slips from the absolute best magazines in the country.

One day, I thought of an idea and I said, *That's not really a story. That's a play.* I didn't know that the dialogue had been very good in my stories, but the narrative was terrible. That was pointed out to me later. Someone then could have saved me a lot of time. I started writing it as a play, and within half-a-page I'd become a playwright.

Richard Greenberg

When I was just starting, I wrote plays very quickly, in order to get into Yale, because at the time I applied you needed two plays and I'd only written one. I just kept writing plays quickly, and I was constantly ripping off Lanford Wilson so blatantly that I'm sure it was actionable. Luckily, none of those plays ever got produced.

Douglas Carter Beane

During the day, I would work at the Drama Book Shop as a clerk, and that way I could read plays for free. They have a great policy since people all the time would want monologues or suggestions for plays. I could take the plays home at night, and I just had to return them—put them back on the shelf. So, I'd take a play every night and read it.

That was my education. I just read.

And the great thing about that was that if I had gone to a college where I was taught writing, someone would have pointed out the really great plays. I had to discover them myself—to get to *Strange Interlude* you have to read *Marco Millions*. That was fascinating. It was a great way for me to learn. It was my particular path. I don't recommend anyone else take it.

It was ten years before I wrote anything, but that's the way I did it.

Lisa Kron

I spent the early 1980s working in the performance-art scene in the East Village, but became more and more interested in taking my performances and making them into theatre. In particular, I was doing solo work, and I was very interested in the inherent problems of making a solo performance into a play. Where do you get dramatic action if there's no one else onstage with you? I then focused my efforts into that.

Paula Vogel

I had an older brother who died from AIDS, who was quite brilliant. He was supposed to be the writer in the family: wrote novels, wrote poetry. And you know how, in a family, as siblings, you never do what your older sibling is doing?

I started thinking about theatre as not as literary a form as the novel or as a poem. I started telling myself that playwriting was actually not writing, that it was all right to write a play because, basically, I was writing the script—but that actors and directors would actually be writing the production. So, I wasn't really a writer. I was writing a scenario. I was writing a structure. I was writing an excuse for us all to get together in a room.

Wendy Wasserstein

When I was a child, I used to take dance class at June Taylor's School of Dance, and I quickly realized that I didn't have a career on *The Jackie Gleason Show*. Then, in high school, I learned that you could get out of sports by writing something called "The Mother–Daughter Fashion Show." Those were the first scenes and little plays that I wrote.

John Pielmeier

I started out as an actor. I left grad school and went right into a professional acting job, regionally, and worked non-stop for a good number of years. I came to The O'Neill Theater Center as an actor the first time, and at the time I was a writer by hobby. I came to the O'Neill and totally fell in love with that process. The image, although it is not literally true, is walking back into my apartment in New York and pulling out a typewriter, and starting to write—because I found it so exciting.

Charles Busch

Right out of college, I started doing a one-man show because I couldn't afford to have actors. I decided, *I at least have myself.* So, I wrote all this material. I was very industrious, and I booked myself all over the country. I would just show up in Indianapolis and find a list of all the nonprofit theatres, and go to an audition in the office. Then, if they liked me, they'd say, "Come back in six months." And I'd show up again. All I needed was a chair. It was just getting the right chairs.

I learned. In a way, really, it was kind of like being in vaudeville in a certain sense. For six years, I did all these solo pieces and learned so much about exposition and characterization. Since I was working on a bare stage, I learned how to establish where I was, what the time of the play was, in an effortless way.

John Pielmeier

I was very unhappy as an actor. I found it emotionally a very difficult life for me to live. So, when the playwriting came along, I said, *Well, I think this is the way to go.*

David Auburn

I started off doing acting, just on an amateur level, in college. And I was performing in a student troupe that wrote Second City–style sketches. But I figured out pretty quickly that I wasn't a very good actor; I was a much better writer, and if I wanted to get laughs in the sketches, I'd better write myself some stuff. I wasn't funny enough to put it across the way some of the other people, who had a natural acting gift, could. For me, it was a question of overcoming a limitation in one area and trying to really do another.

After I moved to New York, I spent a couple of years working different, strange jobs. And I eventually got into this Juilliard program, which was just starting out. Unlike a lot of graduate programs, where I think you're meant to learn playwriting, somehow it was just a residency where you could be at Juilliard, write plays under the supervision of the playwrights who were running the program, Chris Durang and Marsha Norman—fantastic teachers. So, you got the benefit of their wisdom and experience, but mostly you could write plays and have them done by these terrific Juilliard actors.

Douglas Carter Beane

I think a lot of people also become actors first because it is the most visible part of the theatre. I was always fascinated by playwriting and playwrights. I read every play I could get my hands on. When I was a kid and I'd see a movie, I would ask, *Who wrote that?* I always wanted to see WRITTEN BY. I was fascinated to know that somebody wrote *All About Eve.* More than the performances or the design or the direction of the play, I asked, *Who wrote the words?*

Charles Busch

I didn't really want to be a writer, particularly. I just wanted to be onstage and I had to find some way to do it—because the message was getting back to me that I was a little too offbeat or weird. So, I started writing my own material and I became a writer out of necessity and I hope grew into a good writer.

John Patrick Shanley

I rented an apartment out in Green Point, as an office. It was a two-bedroom apartment and it had no furniture except a desk and chairs. And I would go out there and I would write. I was growing basil in one of the bedrooms, just be-cause I felt so guilty about not using the space. I had a basil farm going there.

But after a year, I said to a friend, "I feel like an unwed mother. I feel I'm trapped at home while everybody else is going somewhere." So then, I rented a commercial office. And I would go in, just to have somebody to say "Good morning" to on the way to my own sad little room again. But at least I had that illusion of being part of the work force.

Pamela Gien

I had no idea that I would write something, until I was, about five years ago (ca. 1996), in a class with Larry Moss. He's an extraordinarily gifted teacher. I went in, just as I would go in any other day, and he said, "Turn to the person next to you and tell that person a story." And it could be something that happened to you today, or it could be something that happened a long time ago.

The story of my grandfather's murder came into my mind. And I had really not thought about that for—well, it happened when I was ten. I turned and told the person next to me. It was an extraordinary experience because I began to remember, at ten-years old, what my thought process was in the car coming home from my grandfather's funeral.

And Larry said, "The second part of the exercise is to stage the story that you just told." I went away and thought, *Oh, my gosh, how will I do this?* I didn't know many black South African actors in Los Angeles at the time. So, I thought, *Well, what I'll do is just play around with the dialects and the parts myself and see what happens. I'll just bring it in as an improv class.*

And I did, absolutely shaking from head to toe. I had never been able to talk about who I am, really. To stand up as myself was the most frightening experience. I thought, for sure, everybody would say, "This is the stupidest thing," or "What is this?" People stood up and were weeping and applauding, and I thought I had gone mad.

Nicky Silver

I was aware of the theatre in the 1970s. Nineteen-seventy-nine or 1980 would be the formative years of my theatrical mind. And I think the theatre was much riskier then, to be perfectly honest. If you look back on what was being produced and what was being seen by a big cross-section of the public, I think it was much more daring, and that's where I got my aesthetic.

John Weidman

I had gone to the theatre my whole life, and my happiest times were spent at the theatre. But it was never my intention to have a career in the theatre at all. I didn't act in high-school plays. I was sort of a serious kid. I thought I would become a politician.

And my Dad, who was primarily a novelist, really only worked in the theatre for four or five years. But he saw writing as a way to make your way through life, and did not encourage my brother or me to follow in his footsteps in any way. In fact, he was pleased we weren't.

I wound up at law school, in the early '70s, which was still the '60s, and was sort of aimlessly drifting—we didn't worry a lot about what we were going to do five years from now, five minutes from now, in the '60s. I looked at law school and I thought, *I don't want to be a lawyer. This is not for me. What could I do right here, right now?* And I thought, *You know, you could sit in the Yale Law School Library with a legal pad and a pen, and write a play.* I knew what a play looked like. You put the characters' name in boldface and then you write what they say underneath, and then something comes after that.

So, I did it with the innocence that you have when you don't know that you don't know what you're doing. I just did it. I finished it and I sent it to Hal Prince, whom I had met through my Dad, and he decided to do it—which even now seems crazy.

Keith Glover

In my ignorance, I thought you could just send a play and they go, "Oh, this is great, you know let's do it," or not do it. And I sent [the first draft of *Dancing on Moonlight*] in. And the Public Theater sent me a letter back: we are not interested in doing this play. And then I thought, *OK, this is a challenge.* And I went back into writing it.

Harvey Fierstein

I was working as a performer, and I was working with a lot of playwrights and somebody asked, "Why don't you write a play?" And I said, "Well, I can't spell." And somebody said the most important thing that was ever said to me—of course, there's SpellCheck and things like that—but at that time, somebody said, "There are people that get about four dollars an hour who will fix your spelling. You go ahead and write."

That's advice I still actually give out.

August Wilson

I started my career as a poet on April 1, 1965. Poetry, for me, is the highest form of literary art. So, of course, naturally, that's what I wanted to do. And I spent the better part of ten, fifteen years trying to write a line the equal of John Berryman's "I saw nobody coming, so I went instead," which to me is still the greatest line of poetry I read.

When I started my career in earnest, in 1979, I realized that I had something and I had all these years of writing poetry. Someone I ran into said, "A definition of poetry is 'the enlargement of the sayable.'" And I had all that. The poem is the distillation of ideas into basically images and using metaphors and things of that sort. So, when I started writing the plays, underneath all the plays and my years of training is a poet.

John Patrick Shanley

I'd been a poet for many years and nobody cared. And I wrote a play, and everybody got together and built scenery, and learned their lines and put on costumes. And I said, *Well, this is significantly better.*

Mary Rodgers

I started writing children's songs for Little Golden Records when I was twenty-one or twenty-two. Those were my first paying jobs, which were actually for hire. I didn't ask for royalties because I didn't know any better—and you'd think I would, considering who my father (Richard Rodgers) was. He knew about royalties!

My mother and father both would say, "People will take you at the price you put on yourself. If you keep doing these three-hundred-dollar songs, they'll think you're just cheap." And I said, "Yeah, but they'll hire me because if I don't do it that way, there will be nine-hundred other people competing for the job."

Paula Vogel

I was in high school and there was a drama class. I was fourteen- or fifteen-years old. I wandered in. They were doing *The Skin of Our Teeth,* and I thought, *I never want to be outside this room again.*

2

Writing for the Stage

Edward Albee

The trick is to try to write a play, actor-proof and director-proof, critic-proof and audience-proof.

Nilo Cruz

For me, fear has to do with facing the blank page—not knowing what I am going to write about.

Harvey Fierstein

We, as writers, we talk so much about the empty page and that challenge. But for me, the challenge is that voice in my head that just makes me crazy until I finally write it down.

Robert Anderson

It's usually three years between the time I finish a play and the time it gets on. It's murder.

Edward Albee

I keep a play in my head for years before I trust it to the page. I let it evolve.

Keith Glover

I usually get the title first and I usually run it past my wife and I ask, "What do you think about this?" And she goes, "OK. You can do a little bit better," or something like that. And then, I try to live up to the title.

Theresa Rebeck

Sometimes, I'll see someone in an orange sweater and think, *Oh, a person in an orange sweater. Her name might be this.* It's the mystery of where ideas come from.

Nilo Cruz

I usually start with something it could be. It could be just a face, a character, it could be a name. It could be some particular kind of behavior that I'm interested in exploring. So, I never know what the play is going to be about.

Theresa Rebeck

You have to center yourself deep inside the body of the character, so the words can rise out of that.

Marsha Norman

[Director] Jon Jory said, "I can just tell you the mistakes you don't have to make as a first-time writer." And then, he especially gave me a great piece of advice: "When you're looking for a subject, look to a time in your life when you were terrified—when you were really frightened, when you were scared, when you were frozen in fear." And that does, indeed, turn out to be a great place to look for subject matter.

Nicky Silver

I don't think anything I do is either risky or safe. I don't think you can think about it. You're so lucky, you feel so happy to have a germ of an idea. You can't say, *Oh, too damn risky,* or, *Too damn safe.* You're just happy that something came that day. It's just an expression of your unconscious more than anything else.

Edward Albee

By the time a play moves from the unconscious to my aware-
ness of it, it's already begun to exist. And then I let it develop
to the extent that it wants to, until it wants to be written
down. I write nothing down. I don't take notes. I don't write
scenes down.

Suheir Hammad

It lives inside of you until you write it down. Our experience
with the show [*Russell Simmons Presents Def Poetry Jam*]
has been that all of these poems that we're performing come
from personal experiences. They were reactions to the things
that were going on around us. Often, they were what was
missing in what the world was telling us about ourselves.
And as a poet, you carry this around with you until it comes
out. Not fully formed; but it comes out in a shape that you
can then edit and manipulate, either for the page or for
the stage.

It's all personal experience, which if you do not say will
make you sick. It'll stay inside of you.

Samm-Art Williams

Poetry is personal. Someone might read your poem and not
get what you intended. With a play, it has to be dramatized

and the audience has to relate to this poem you are writing. What makes it work is its simplicity.

August Wilson

My plays tend to have metaphors, they tend to have images. The approach to them is the approach of a poet, in terms of the certain ways of thinking and trying to find the core essence and idea that you want to communicate.

Nilo Cruz

Writing for the stage has to be musical, the writing must be rhythmic.

Richard Greenberg

There's the rhythm you hear in your head. I write for my own ear. I know exactly, as I'm writing, how it's meant to sound.

Lanford Wilson

I'm not just turning inward and escaping with my plays. I'm wasting my time if my plays don't make comments on contemporary society.

Douglas Carter Beane

I understand the cohesiveness that some playwrights talk about. But I personally like collaboration. It's why I chose to be a playwright. If I wanted to be in total control, I would write a novel.

Brian Clark

If, as a writer, you want to have the whole shooting match, you should be writing novels. You can write them like Ivy Compton-Burnett, which are all dialogue, if you want to. But the fact is the joy of theatre and the whole point of theatre is, first of all, that it's a social art that's shared among a group of people—including an audience. Secondly, it is the art above all that investigates conflict.

Jonathan Tolins

I'm quickly learning that one of the most important tools a playwright must have is to be able to filter out the voices that he or she should not listen to for a second.

Eve Merriam

Writers tend to be too accommodating. When writing books, people either read them and like them or not. They never come to you afterward and ask, "Why don't you change this character to a man?" or "Have you thought about setting it in Iowa?"

Brian Clark

The main education of a playwright occurs in the theatre and in the rehearsal room.

August Wilson

Craft can be self-taught because there are so many brilliant examples in terms of playwriting. The craft is all around you. Just go to the library, pick up Chekhov if you want to know about craft. The examples are there.

Marsha Norman

The play is not meant to exist on the page. It's not a manuscript in that way. What you need to do is hear it. And then, you need to get the response from the other people in the room. You need to see what it is. You need to let it rise up off the print, to see what you have.

But it happens a lot that young writers will revise—they'll be so eager to hear from someone, they'll take it next door, in the middle of the night, and say, "Read this." And then, the person next door will say, "Well, I don't know. I think you should make the brother a dog." And then the [young playwright will say], "Well, you know, that's good. I'll go do it."

And so, before anybody has even had a chance to hear it or see it or read it, a rewrite is in the works. And that's a mess for kids.

August Wilson

I don't mind cutting. I'll throw out half, keep the four pages. But it has to be the right four pages. And a lot of times, people don't always know, because they're not sure exactly why a certain thing is there, why it's said a certain way. So, you do have to keep it, for the musicality or for the meaning. For instance, there was a line, a guy says, "I've seen people beat up love." And somebody says, "Cut that." I say, "No, I'm not going to cut that 'beat up love' line." I'll cut some other stuff; but there's something about that. It's an idea.

Arthur Kopit

Story is told through a form. So you have to know the story, and then you allow the story to guide you to what the form of it is supposed to be.

August Wilson

Very often in my plays is this: putting the culture onstage and demonstrating its ability to sustain black Americans. In doing that, there's a lot of storytelling. It's just a part of the culture, coming out of an oral tradition, a way of passing along information. And of course, in order to keep the information alive, if you make this story, you want to make it memorable so that someone would then go and repeat it and repeat it, over and over. And the information is kept alive.

That's the first responsibility of storytellers, to make a story memorable, so that it can be passed along.

Samm-Art Williams

If you are a writer, what you choose to write about has nothing to do with the color of your skin. Black is not a nationality. White is not a nationality. We're Americans. We write about the American experience.

If people expect me only to write about the Black Experience, that is their problem.

Peter Parnell

It may be that I'm trying to find something that I don't understand, which the process of writing is trying to help me to understand. And it usually isn't until the end of a first draft, way later, that I will say, *Oh, well, I guess that's what this play is sort of about.* Then, the rewriting will be to help me get to make that better, toward what it is.

Jonathan Tolins

I don't write until there's something to write. I know there probably are some very disciplined playwrights who get up every morning and have a cup of coffee or, Tennessee Williams in his bathrobe, who would write every morning for a few hours. I feel the writing is not the hard part, it's having something worth writing that's difficult. So really, it's just developing a gestation period. And I keep busy doing other things that provide an income, in between the times when I'm ready to write a play.

Theresa Rebeck

I worked in Hollywood for a while, on a sitcom, and it was one of the most psychotic experiences in my life. I didn't know what I was getting into at all. I would go home, and I wouldn't be able to get out of bed in the morning. I would sit in a room, terrified. And I kept thinking, *I know there's a play here. This is just too strange a world for there not to be a play here.*

Charles Busch

With comedy, it's just your hunch. It's not even necessarily a line that you think is particularly funny—and you've worked it out methodically, it has all the right elements, it should get them laughing. It's just a hunch. And it's so thrilling, every time, the very first time you hear a play read aloud, at the very first reading. And you think, *Oh yeah, that one. They got that one. They got that laugh. Ooh, ooh, ooh, they didn't get that one. That was a bad one.* But it is really thrilling.

Douglas Carter Beane

I happen to like the smaller casts because they do remind us that theatre is a very tribal event.

Edward Albee

My plays tend to have small casts. It's probably not the limitation of the stage as much as it is the limitation of my mind. I don't know what to do with eighteen different characters wandering around. I'd be happier dealing with three or four that I could handle—that won't be tripping all over each other.

Theresa Rebeck

I'm always fascinated by conflict or situation or people; and then, I work it through until what I would call the deeper subject emerges.

George Faison

Sometimes, a writer will write something that fits perfectly in one mouth. And then, there are other things that resonate and ricochet because there are many voices and attitudes involved in one speech.

Edward Albee

I made an experiment once, when I was writing *Who's Afraid of Virginia Woolf?* And I was in the first act, because I write my plays from beginning to ending, which is sometimes unusual, but I do. I got an idea for something that I thought would be good in the third act, which as you know, in *Virginia Woolf*, is a long, long way from the first act. And so, I wrote down about a four-page scene, and I put it away.

I went back and finished the first act.

Couple of months later, I got to act 3, and I remembered that I had written that scene. I looked at it and I liked it a lot. It was really good writing. I tried to put in in the play. It wouldn't go. The characters would not say it—because I had written it down too damn soon. That simple.

David Ives

I couldn't work like Albee. I'm not so either sure of myself or so . . . I don't know, I don't have the same attachment to what I've written to think that's right. I will change absolutely anything.

Timothy Mason

I tend to hear someone speaking and then, about a year-and-a-half later, start writing the play.

I take very few notes. I used to, when I was younger. I kept recipe-card boxes full of notes. And that was a wonderful way for me to work at that time. And now, it doesn't seem to be.

Nilo Cruz

I'm interested in beauty. I find that sometimes I've gotten comments, "Well, people don't speak that way." And I say, "I'm certainly not interested in having the kind of language that one hears in a bodega, in a grocery store." To me, that's not art. We're writing for the stage, and I think to have beauty on the stage you have to be courageous.

Arthur Kopit

When you write a play, there's dialogue. But I've always felt—and I try to tell playwrights that I'm teaching—the dialogue is the least of it, absolute least of it. Too much dependence upon talk gets you nowhere.

Charles Busch

To grow as a writer, I had to write a play that I wasn't in, because as a performer, I have a very specific thing that I do.

Alfred Uhry

One wonderful thing about working in the theatre is you could write a play and three weeks later you can have people sit around and read it. If you write a movie, it's probably going to be eleven years until something happens. And by then, you've forgotten what you were doing in the first place.

Paul Rudnick

I used to have—I still do have—this fear, when I am very early in the playwriting process, when I do a first draft, I used to think, *Oh, my God, every line should be perfect before you continue on to the next perfect line.* Then, I realized that would mean I would write one play every three-thousand years. So, I would just spew out a first draft, just get it on the page: just get it over with.

And then, I would have this terror that I would be killed that night in a car accident, and that people would find this first draft and imagine that I thought it was good. It finally occurred to me, if that should happen, I would be dead— Why am I worrying?

And I met another playwright who was not really a very good playwright, but one of the most confident human beings I've ever met. And she was so sure of her own genius that at the end of each day of writing, she would put the pages she'd worked on in the freezer, so in case her apartment caught on fire, they would be saved—or at least chilled.

Harvey Fierstein

I wrote my first play, and the *Village Voice* in their review compared me to the devil come to earth—and I knew I was on to something.

Diana Son

I think people assume that I'm writing autobiographically—and then feel stunned and betrayed when they find out that I'm not. *Stop Kiss* is about these two women who fall in love, and they kiss, and they get beat up. And people would come to me afterward, "Did that happen to you?" Or then, there is the assumption that I was gay.

I was hurt by it, actually hurt and shocked, because I assumed that since I was a writer, that people were counting on me to use my imagination.

Christopher Durang

When I wrote *Sister Mary Ignatius Explains It All for You,* I'd had a writer's block for about two years; and my mother was dying of cancer, which was very sad. And I was no longer a believer in the Catholic faith I was brought up in. I felt very disoriented, because watching my mother's illness, I wished I were a believer.

By the way, I'm not actually an atheist. I'm sort of a supermarket agnostic, whatever that means. But from that I thought back on my religious upbringing. And I thought, *When I grew up in that, there was an answer for absolutely everything.* My impulse went from that to, *I want to write a play in which a representative of the Catholic Church comes out and explains everything.*

Timothy Mason

The Fiery Furnace, I think, began when I was living in Minneapolis and had a friend who co-founded a shelter for battered women, one of the first in that city. And she'd come by my apartment and tell me stories from work. And she would sort of unwind. When she left, I would be like this, because the stories were truly horrific.

I got permission to spend a night in the shelter, because I said, *I've got to write about this.* And that was a very rough night. I came away from it knowing that I couldn't write about it because I would be writing about an issue. And I didn't want to write a TV movie of the week.

So, I let it go for a long time, maybe ten or twelve years. And that Wisconsin farm woman began speaking to me in my head. And it turned out not to be a play about the abuse of women, although that figures in it, but a play about women and the choices that were offered to them in an earlier era.

Roberto Aguirre-Sacasa

Every year, I would see six or seven plays by Shakespeare—really beautiful productions. And I think I learned more about a kind of contemporary storytelling watching those plays—and watching those productions—than I did from any other or any other playwright.

Shakespeare had ghosts. Shakespeare had monsters—his epic form: low- and high-culture elements, which is something that I do.

I draw on novelists. I draw on comic books. I draw on movies, soap operas. All that gets filtered into my work somehow. I think unconsciously, I don't set out to put in all those elements. And frequently in fact say, *OK, I'm going to write a play. No monsters. No gay characters.* And pretty soon, there's a kid who's creating a Frankenstein monster, and the Frankenstein monster's gay in his bedroom.

But it's funny when my parents go to see my plays. They can see every movie that I saw growing up—"Oh, it's just like in *Clash of the Titans.*"

Daisy Foote

People are getting more worried about selling tickets. They're thinking, *Well, maybe if we made theatre more like movies.* And it's a dangerous, slippery slope to get on.

David Ives

I think you have to be a fool to write for the theatre these days without regard for the economics of the theatre.

Brian Clark

All English playwrights write for television, as far as I know, as well as the theatre. Stoppard, Brenton, Hare, Griffiths, and so on. We all work with the same actors and directors in television as in the theatre. It's a much healthier, much happier scene altogether.

Douglas Carter Beane

Why do I choose to write theatre, when certainly I can write a movie and make so much more money and have a really nice house, and really have super-sexy friends with really great names?

I love it. It's my life.

The thing about film writing, and I've done it about six times now and gearing toward seven, the thing about film writing is that there are thousands of people who live in Los Angeles County and their job is to save your writing. It is their job to make it better, to make it palatable, to make it less special. That's their job. And I have meetings and meetings and meetings where people will tell me how to make it less unique. So, when I hear things like, *That's where our focus is, in movies,* even in something like independent films—which I feel off-Broadway has become, the equivalent of independent films—even in independent films, which are really the movies anyone with a thought in their head would go see, there are meetings where people will say, "Cut that."

You finally get through all that garbage, all the people saying, "Cut this. No one will like that. No one will get that." You get to the screening, the sneak-preview screening, and there are cards. And these cards can say we don't like the ending. And they will go and re-shoot a new ending to the movie.

This is unbelievable.

We don't do this in the theatre. If people feel a little let down by the ending of the play, that's OK. I want them to be a little let down. It is about an artist and creative person telling you the life they've lived. It's not about, *This is how we've cleaned it up and made it palatable, and made money off of it.*

Paul Rudnick

One of the most wonderful things about the theatre is that alone among the media there can be less censorship since the writers have far more legal controls over it. The Dramatists Guild of America contract means that no one can change a word of your work without your permission.

Douglas Carter Beane

As a gay white man, I think gay sensibility is a major part of theatre. It has always been a part of theatre. It has always been a voice that's heard, even when we didn't know it. I tend to write gay characters in my plays just because I'm always on the side of the outsider. I like the person who doesn't have the world handed to him. It's also my voice.

Bill Russell

It's very important to me as a writer to try and give gay characters life, so that other people won't feel as out of it as I did.

Paula Vogel

There are particular challenges to writing female characters in the 20th century. I think that every male character comes onstage carrying behind him the legacy of Hamlet, whereas women characters are fighting against the legacy of Linda Loman or Gertrude, or the secondary roles, and that's something that's there. It doesn't necessarily mean by sex that one can write great female characters. To me, the greatest writers of female characters are Chekhov, Tennessee Williams, and John Guare. But as a woman, I want to be very careful to try and add to the legacy that I've been given for actresses in the future.

John Weidman

When the Roundabout decided to do *Assassins,* I went back and I looked at the script—and I hadn't looked at it for, I don't know, seven or eight years really. And I read it, and I got so depressed. I thought, *God, I used to be so talented, and now I don't know what I'm doing.*

I went back to my computer and I found the early drafts of it, in which the scenes were twice as long and they were filled with terrible things—and I immediately perked up.

Arthur Kopit

The Dramatists Guild had a gala in the spring. And the event that they showed for the people who were there was a series of what are called *outtakes*. Included were an outtake from *Fiddler on the Roof;* a scene from Marsha Norman; David Henry Hwang did a scene; Arthur Miller did an outtake from *The Crucible.* And I was so proud to be a member of the Dramatists Guild and to be a playwright because every single one of those scenes was wonderful.

And I thought, *These writers absolutely, without hesitation, cut a scene that you would give your eyeteeth to write.* Not because the scene was no good; but because the scene didn't help the show in the long run. They knew.

I wish other playwrights could have seen what good writers cut from their pieces.

Scott Elliott

I worked with Arthur Miller and he was totally great about cutting his own work. I had no problem with him. We sat down around the table with the cast and I just said, "Let's get rid of that." "OK, get rid of that."

Richard Greenberg

Any play that's worth anything is worth cutting. Because the more you cut, the more you get to what's there. And all those lovely phrases that mean nothing come out.

David Ives

I've taught playwriting and I always tell my students that the only true thing I've ever heard said about playwriting is from

George S. Kaufman: plays are not written, plays are rewritten.

And yet, I have to have something that I think is as good as I can get it before I show it to anybody. I can't imagine, for example, the process of coming up and just writing for two weeks. That's inconceivable to me. I have to lock myself away for a long time and come up with something that is ready to be shown to someone else. And then, I need lots of other ideas. And I fix according to that.

Arthur Kopit

You can't edit yourself; and yet, you are editing yourself. You're watching what's good and what's not good. But it's not on the basis of, *What will the audience say?* You're saying, *Is this honest or not?* It's a constant dialogue with yourself.

Alfred Uhry

It's a discipline, like a dancer working his muscles or an athlete keeping in shape. You have to try to distance yourself from being afraid when you're hearing material read, or you'll never learn anything.

You have to become as cold and as hard about your material, or even more so, than you are about other people's material.

It's not always a success. It's something, I imagine, like taking class every day if you're a dancer. It's hard to do and it never gets easy. But if you don't do it, I don't think you're a professional. You're not really a professional writer because you're just in love with your words.

The effect on other people is what matters—not what matters to you.

David Auburn

That first reading, really, that's the most suspenseful moment in the entire process for me, more than going in before an audience for the first time. Because essentially, I never really know until I hear the first reading. *Is this play basically interesting to people?*

Richard Greenberg

You just want to see the experience extended, beyond the page. It's quite wonderful when it's beautifully embodied.

Terrence McNally

This great act of will to assemble people, sit in a room, put the lights down, and tell them a story—to think we can hold their interest—that takes great courage.

Charles Busch

Nothing is scarier than a laugh that dies in a Broadway house.

Michael Frayn

When you're up against it, as I am, struggling with a new play, I realize I don't know anything about playwriting whatsoever.

Arthur Kopit

The most exciting part is in the writing, when something is happening. Or it can be in collaboration, in rehearsal, when something has suddenly emerged. It's when you no longer know who gave an idea; or it's a line and an actor does something, and then you see something you didn't see. And something happens there, and you say, *Oh my God, look what that can do.* Or when I'm writing, and suddenly it takes over and I say, *Wow.* Then, the piece is up and I say, *Oh, thank God, it resembles what I want and the audience is moved.*

3

Musical Theatre

John Guare

A play is one thing. But a musical is like a great Erector Set, a great contraption, where you have to solve problems immediately, writing in a sort of semaphore style.

Greg Kotis

I am not at all a poet. The process of writing lyrics to me was very much like doing a crossword puzzle.

Douglas Carter Beane

Musical theatre is a style unto itself. It is a form. It is an art form. I find it has been a delight for me to write a book of a musical comedy, and get to know all the rules and read everything everyone's written on it.

John Kander

I fell in love with opera. Listening to those Saturday broadcasts somehow or other implanted the idea that music telling a story was about the most exciting thing that you could be involved with.

Eve Merriam

I love writing for the musical theatre because you have collaborators and can always blame everything on them if things don't work out. Writing for the straight theatre is something that terrifies me.

Martin Charnin

When I wrote with Richard Rodgers, I never collaborated with him. You did not collaborate with Richard Rodgers. You would simply sit and put together what, in essence, was a finished lyric—turn it over to Dick. And two days later, the melody would come back. You would, of course, fine-tune it. But it was not a collaboration in the sense of the true kind of working collaboration that Charles Strouse and I have.

Jeanine Tesori

The hard thing about falling into a writing marriage is to bypass that, *Oh, I love you, I love you,* to, *Oh, my god, you have spinach in your teeth—look!* Right to that immediacy of, *I really don't think this works. I think that works.*

Arthur Kopit

I've always loved musicals. I've always loved plays. They do different things. There's some material that can be a play, and it can be a musical; but you have to ask yourself, *Well, is this a musical and what is it going to express that you couldn't express without music?*

I think you have to have an instinctive sense of how a musical's story unfolds, as opposed to a play's story. There are just certain aspects—they're not rules, but there's a way the major elements are going to be sung, or they're in music; or else, why is it a musical? And the reason for that is not because the audience is there to be entertained, but because the emotion is so great that it can't be expressed only in words.

Fred Ebb

You couldn't study lyric writing in school or I would have. I love theatre. I used to go and see everything. And I knew every song from every show. It's what I wanted, except I knew I didn't have any composing skill.

Tony Kushner

Caroline, or Change, felt to me like a story, which would need to access a certain level of emotion in the audience and a depth of feeling in the audience since, in some ways, it's a play about loss and mourning: sad, difficult things that words alone are not going to get at. I think it immediately began to feel like something that music would be necessary for. So, I started writing it in loosely rhymed verse, and always with the idea in mind that I would find the right composer for it.

John Guare

A musical is much more a joint effort, in a sense like working on a movie. When you're writing a movie, you have to scale back your writing because you just say, *Well, the camera will take care of this description, the camera will do this. And it'll get too much of* muchness *if I write it.* It's the same way with a composer. You say, *I have to write this back because the music will take care of this.* But you have to write what the scene will be and write the intention of the song.

Marvin Hamlisch

It's something that you have to really love to do it because to write a show—everyone thinks is the easiest thing in the world. And to put it on, you think, *Oh, that's a piece of cake,* and when you have a hit, *Wow.* For all of those moments, there are other moments when the show never happens, the show is a bomb, all those other things that you live with, that you don't put in your bio.

August Wilson

I've had actors stand up onstage and say my words, and it feels good. But in *King Hedley II,* there's a scene and there's a waltz. Leslie Uggams is there sitting, and we have the music for the waltz. And it came up, *Well, maybe if she had a few words, she could sing.* So, I wrote four lines—it took me forever.

So, I'm sitting there in the theatre, and she starts singing these four lines that I wrote. And it was the most glorious experience I've ever had. And I said, *Hey, I want to write some more of this,* because just four lines were just wonderful. I want to do that.

I think that the musical theatre is the American contribution to world theatre. The musical and blues is the music indigenous to the continent.

Susan Birkenhead

If the composer is a dramatist, which Jule Styne certainly was and Charles Strouse certainly is, then somehow or other it's mostly right—and then we collaborate. I'll take the music, and by and large set a lyric to it and at least get going with it. Then, we get into the room together and iron it out. Henry Krieger prefers to have the lyric first, and that's a great luxury. But again, we get into the room together and we pull back and forth, and twist.

Bill Russell

We usually are writing for a character, but we don't always know what actor will play that character or what his or her vocal range is: what key it should be in, for instance. And we do end up fine-tuning these things in rehearsals and readings since different actors have different vocal qualities that you want to try to accentuate, to give the best vocal shot and to make your song land best in his or her vocal range.

Don Schlitz

Writing for a country-music audience has been a great learning ground for me because the point of a country song is to write conversationally—that it could be something that someone would say to someone else.

Charles Strouse

If I suggested literary ideas to Alan Jay Lerner, he was receptive. But I noticed the pencil never came out. He would listen. But he went home to a little closet and then wrote and wrote and wrote, and would call me up with a lyric. And very often, I'm critical, and I would be with him. He would say, "Yes, yes, I see," and go back to the closet. But he would not write in front of me.

Jeff Marx

Usually, the composer writes the music and the lyricist writes the lyrics. But we (and Robert Lopez), actually—Bobby writes music and lyrics, and I write music and lyrics. So we decided, early on, just to try sitting in a room together and hashing it all out. We don't split things up. We don't work on anything individually. We don't bring in ideas because then somebody works on something for four hours and brings it in, the other person goes, "Oh, I don't love it." You go, "What do you mean? I worked for four hours on this. How could you not like it that quickly?" So, we work on everything together at the same time, in the same room, and we only keep what we both like.

John Guare

We had this idea of playing *Two Gentlemen of Verona* out on the street, this noisy street—and it was a summer of great racial unrest and turmoil. *How would people listen to this exquisite poetry?*

We got this great idea that Galt MacDermot, who composed *Hair,* was going to be a resident composer that year—just fortuitous, he was there and he was going to write some incidental music for it. We said, "Wouldn't it be funny if the songs acted as subtitles before the speeches?" So that the audience would know what the meaning of the scene was; it wouldn't be put off by the poetry and it being Shakespeare. And so a couple of songs grew into thirty songs, again, by being sparked by the cast.

And then it moved into the park and got great reviews, and then moved to Broadway. The main problem was I had to give it a much more formal opening. And the greatest problem was writing a formal opening.

Marvin Hamlisch

There has been a change in theatre, a major change. Possibly starting with the British Invasion—I don't know how long it's going to stay. But we had, for a while, these through-composed shows, which drove me crazy because I really didn't want people to start singing about, "I want some water / How is your daughter?"

It's interesting, when you see a revival and you see what the old-type show was, we're kind of out of that, too. We've grown past that, about the little book with the wonderful great songs, one after another. Yet, where the pendulum swung got a little bit too crazy. I used to love going to shows—the great shows such as *My Fair Lady, Fiddler on the Roof, West Side Story*—where not only did you have these great melodies and lyrics, but there would be a scene, or there would be a sentence, or there would be a moment.

For instance what I'm writing now, I like the idea that yes, if I needed to take something from the book, if I said, *This is going to be a great song, I've got to take it,* you have to have a book writer who says, "It's OK. I can live with that." On the other hand, I'm one of the few writers who says, "I love this so much, I don't want to touch this. This is better spoken than it will ever by sung."

I have always felt that some of these through-composed shows are through-composed because the books are not very good. And I have noticed in the theatre that people don't cough during songs. People tend to cough during scenes. So, if you keep singing the whole time, the chances are you eradicate the coughing.

4

The Workshop and Development

Terrence McNally

There's nothing wrong with the workshop and development. But I think very often they become an excuse not to do the play.

Richard Nelson

There's a question of what a workshop is for. I've worked at the studio at the Royal National Theatre, doing a workshop. It was very, very useful. But no one from the theatre ever saw what we did. It was only for us. And that was a very useful thing, only for us, to get people together to try to sort something out. It's a problem in a workshop or reading or anything like that if there is an element of judgment over it.

You are doing this workshop to see if something works, and therefore see if you can go to the next step. That's a big problem, and it's a very confusing one for a playwright, because people can't separate what they see in a reading or a workshop from the work itself. If you have Meryl Streep playing the maid in your reading—she'll never play it in a production, but she does the reading—the people say, "Oh, the maid was fantastic." And then, you have another reading in two months and you don't have Meryl Streep, and the people say, "What'd you do to the maid? You should work that up. I remember it so much more vividly."

Tony Kushner

When we did the *Caroline, or Change,* workshop, we had this incredibly great kid, who's now got really tall and much too old to be in the show, a wonderful singer who played one of Caroline's kids. He had never been in a show before. He had never done a workshop before. There was a prayer circle before we did that one sing-through for an audience. And everybody joined hands, and they were starting to pray. And this kid said, "I'd like to do it. Dear Lord, please bless this performance today even if it's only a workshop."

Becky Mode

The workshop process, for me, was valuable. I know it can fold in on itself. It wasn't always valuable. But I felt, again, over time, if I got the same message from people that I trusted, it helped me.

Edward Albee

I'm going to say something rather unpopular. I don't think any play should be presented, gone into rehearsal, produced until it is ready to be seen. I think too many plays are work-shopped and tried out—before they're ready.

Paula Vogel

I have a problem, sometimes, with doing cold-staged readings with wonderful directors and actors because they make my script look too good, and I can't see where the problems are. They fix it through their interpretation. I'm actually a believer in getting friends who are not actors, playwrights particularly, around a table—people who cannot act—to go through the first reading. Then, I see what works and doesn't.

Lawrence Sacharow

When characters are not written clearly, but they're sort of poetic, then the playwright usually has an idea in his head about a characterization that you can't get from reading it. Seeing those kinds of writers stage it in a workshop fashion is very helpful. The tendency is not to pace it well, so it tends to be all on one level. And although you can get a lot of clues, they're not concerned with the overall architecture of the piece and how the rhythms work because they're working more moment to moment.

David Esbjornson

Readings become commercials in a way. There's a pressure to present them in a way that will get producers interested in actually going to the next step.

Don Schlitz

For me, being new in the world of theatre, I've found that the readings we've done, the workshops, have been immeasurably helpful. Without a wealth of experience, it is the first time that I've seen the process work.

David Leveaux

We have a fairly thriving workshop culture [in England]. Attached, for instance, to our Royal National Theatre is a studio, which is dedicated to the development of work, in a workshop situation.

I think that the idea of the endless workshops defusing the original energy of the play, or a piece of work, is a very genuine danger. And I think it comes from a misplaced notion of refinement.

A word that I particularly hate, which you don't hear so much in the theatre—you hear it more, I think, in the movies—is *polish*. I hate this word because what it conjures up is the notion that somehow you can burnish off the sort of awkward corners and edges of this thing until it becomes acceptable, in a rather homogenized fashion.

In reality, we're all about making a piece of live theatre. And there is only one test that I ever think of applying to that, which is, simply, is it living or is it not living?

Joseph Stein

The workshop experience, by the way, does take some of the burden of the financial pressure off since the producer only has to pay for that workshop, not for a big, fat, four-million-dollar production. They can pay one-hundred-thousand and take a look. For a big musical, with a cast of thirty-five, you're getting a bargain.

Julia Jordan

My experience has been that when you have a workshop that is in front of an audience, as I had with *Tatjana in Color* at Actor's Studio Free Theater, it can be great. When you look at the audience and they're fidgeting or they're not laughing when you [want them to], that's when you know, *OK, I have to look at this piece.*

Rob Ashford

We were fortunate enough to get to do a production of *Thoroughly Modern Millie* in La Jolla. After that experience, I'm a firm believer in that even more advantageous than a workshop is actually to do a production in front of people—normal people that come in.

Lisa Kron

I worked with Paula Vogel as an actor, workshopping *Mineola Twins,* and it was amazing to watch her ruthlessly cut her play. And she said to me, "Never hang onto poetry for its own sake."

Joseph Stein

I don't think a workshop solves all our problems, or even many of our problems, but at least we can get a sense of where the problems are. The only time we really know is when we're in front of a paying audience.

John Tillinger

The classic story is the one of *A Funny Thing Happened on the Way to the Forum,* where nobody laughed. Nobody laughed until they stuck that song into the top of the show. And that happened on the road. That cannot happen in a workshop because everybody's trying to sell the show and then the people who put their money into the show say, "I don't want a thing changed. That's what I want." And so, the creative juices stop flowing.

Lanford Wilson

A playwright is in no shape to hear a word the first time [at a reading]—also, there are thirty-five or forty people listening, and you're saying, *Why did they laugh at that? That isn't funny;* or, *Why didn't they laugh at that?* There were three or four comments that I just didn't hear, they were little rumblings. Everyone was saying, "Oh, that was marvelous; I didn't understand that long speech." I didn't hear any of those comments.

Later, listening to the recording, I heard them. But Marshall (Mason) was the naysayer. He said, "Well, we'll talk later." I thought, *Oh my God.* I did have a chip on my shoulder. I went into that meeting with you and with Milan Stitt, who was the dramaturg on the play, with a real chip on my shoulder because I thought that I'd written a play that was pretty darn good. And either Marshall was more diplomatic than he's ever been known to be, or else he'd really prepared very well and knew what he was talking about, because within a minute or two I was saying, "Well, that is interesting," and writing down little notes on the side of the script.

John Rando

After two weeks of work, Neil Simon came from Los Angeles to see a run-through of *The Dinner Party*, which, frankly, did not go that well. The actors and I had developed some new staging and some things that we thought we were improving.

He very candidly—and in a remarkable way, and I think it happens in any craft—related a story of when he was a boy and loved balsa-wood airplanes, and flew them. He said sometimes he would sand them to make them fly better. And sometimes, he would keep sanding and sanding; and then, they wouldn't fly at all.

That is also another thing about the process, that sometimes you have to write this whole new scene and throw things out—it's making that balsa-wood plane fly. And then, sometimes the rough edges help it.

Julie Taymor

Our first workshop *(The Lion King)* was a workshop that tested the book and the music—the majority of the music. And it was a sit-down—actor, singer, reading—which was absolutely fundamental to know whether this musical was going to work: because it's not about the visuals; it's about the book, the music, and lyrics.

Jonathan Tolins

I feel that *Twilight of the Golds*, had it gone through a very long workshop process—because it's about issues that everybody gets so angry about and has such clear ideas of how one should present these kinds of things, if at all—would have been flattened out tremendously.

Alfred Uhry

It's very important for a playwright to be able to listen to the reading and not be so frightened that you can't hear anything. You've got to make yourself do that. It's really hard. *Everybody is looking at me.* It's nightmare time.

André Bishop

I began to realize that all of these workshops and readings, and all of that, are good. They are bright lights shining in a bad, old world. But really, the way a writer develops—and it's so obvious, all of you know this—is through having his or her play produced, and produced as well as possible. That's real play development.

5

Actors

David Auburn

Learning how to write for actors is one of the hardest things, I think, for a playwright to do. It's really difficult to be in a place where you have enough freedom to learn what the process is that the actors are going through: what kind of questions the actors ask about the script, and incorporate them.

Arthur Miller

I'm part actor myself, and I know what the difficulties are.

To cut, possibly, to the center of the whole problem: when you cast a play, you're casting human beings whose personalities often will come out through a new characterization, and come out differently from the way it ever appeared before. So you get an actor, for example, who has a wonderful, dark tone, but there are comedic scenes in the play and he has no sense of humor. Then, you begin to labor with that lighter, brighter element in him, and try to invent it.

The playwright then is called upon to patch up his performance by adding or subtracting text. I'm talking now, of course, about a new play, which has never been performed before. Pretty soon, the original text begins to get distorted—no one knows quite when or how—by the injection of material that was written, really, to prop up a performance.

Moisés Kaufman

You learn a lot at auditions, a lot. Because you see all these different textures of different actors doing the same lines, and you learn about what works for the part and what doesn't.

Terrence McNally

I'm a great believer in audition. I'm a playwright, and every great actor I've ever worked with has been willing to audition for a role.

Arthur Kopit

I was working on a show this summer with some people who were not trained as actors. And they thought, *Well, how do I*

do it? What am I acting? And I said, "First of all, you have
no bad habits to break. So, you're at an advantage."

Christopher Durang

I actually don't write with certain actors consciously in
mind. Partially, I wrote an early play, *History of the American
Film*, with Sigourney Weaver in mind, before anybody knew
her. Sigourney and I went to Yale School of Drama together.
And even though she's deservedly had a wonderful career,
her first couple of years she had trouble getting cast because
of how tall she is, how patrician she is—how patrician
she seemed.

I told her I had written *History of the American Film* with
her in mind. Not only that, I even added a joke about the
heroine having to leave the orphanage because she is too tall.
I couldn't get anyone to hire Sigourney in the part—they
came close—and it made her disappointed.

And so, I actually protected myself and my actor friends
by just not consciously writing about them—or, writing with
them in mind.

Michael J. Chepiga

The first day of rehearsal we met in a rehearsal hall, and
everybody went around the table, made introductions. An
actor said, "I'm so-and-so. I play this part." We went
through all the seven parts. And I introduced myself and
said, "I'm Michael Chepiga. I think I'm all of you."

Lanford Wilson

I like actors who listen to other actors onstage.

John Patrick Shanley

I like to have actors read the play out loud. I like other people to be there. Nobody can control the situation then. Either it's playing or it stinks.

David Henry Hwang

I think the actor's role is important because most of us who write plays, we write a lot in rehearsal. We come into situations where, the beginning of rehearsal, we get the play to be as good as we can. But once you hear it and once you start to see it in front of an audience, obviously things change. And consciously or unconsciously—I guess consciously since I'm talking about it—I find myself writing for the actors that have been cast; still trying to hold onto my vision, of course.

Basically, the form is literary but at the same time it is about creating an event. And the event has to do with the particular individuals who we have now decided should inhabit these roles. If there's something that they're better at or they can do more strongly than something else, I have a tendency to then start to move the rewrites in that direction.

Robert Anderson

I love casting. I think that you learn, which is part of the preproduction deal. You learn—whether Actors Equity likes it or not—you learn a great deal about your play by hearing it being read over and over again with different actors.

Edward Albee

I've never had a play ruined in casting when I have had a say in the casting. Playwrights don't even read their contracts half the time. In the first commercial production, the contract specifically says that the playwright has control over casting and the choice of director. When casting goes awry in a commercial production, it is usually because the playwright doesn't have the guts or the knowledge to stand up for the rights of his contract. It's your own play, and whenever you have any degree of control over it, you should exert as much as you can. It's much more fun to go with your own mistakes than with somebody else's.

Christopher Durang

I think that being an actor inside a play can teach you good things about writing as well.

David Auburn

Very few actors are willing to give up laughs in a show. And there were moments in *Proof* in which we (and Mary-Louise

Parker) agreed, *You know, this is becoming a little too Cats-kills—or maybe we could lose the laugh here in exchange for something else.*

Harvey Fierstein

I don't think Arthur Laurents (director of *La Cage aux Folles*) would mind my telling the story. I said, "These roles have to be played by gay people." I don't care—you have the greatest seventeen-year-old actress in the world, she cannot play a grandmother. There's stuff she doesn't know. Life has not taught her yet. And there are stakes, especially in a musical where you don't have a hell of a lot of time for character development; there are things in a gay person's baggage that a gay person would carry onto that stage that I don't have time to explain, which an audience would feel. That is the magic of theatre, of what the actor brings, what the playwright brings, what the audience brings—the marriage.

Lanford Wilson

There are two types of playwrights: those who should never go near a production and have no concept of acting—they are more loyal to their friends who may be acting than to their play. Others are thrilled by the theatre, know what they want, have a very good idea of what will work, and are practical in the theatre.

Douglas Carter Beane

There are playwrights who feel that they should be talking to the actor. I make a point of being supportive and nurturing to actors. But I wouldn't give a note to an actor or tell him what to do. That's the director's place.

Robert Anderson

As I get older, I get the feeling, *What's the use of writing plays if there's no one around to act them?* I'm terribly afraid to say, with the American theatre at the moment, that I seem to be writing plays that call for characters of a certain age level—through no fault of the actors, but there are just not any actors of that age.

Lanford Wilson

I write for actors all the time. But I write and they act. During the rehearsal process, of course, lines are dropped, and you realize that certain actors are so good at conveying something with one word that you don't need the entire next speech. Sometimes, you put it in the published text but leave it out of the production. I often want to print something with brackets around it, saying, "This was dropped, but you may need it."

Richard Greenberg

Casting is the most crucial moment I think. It's where you can go really, really, very badly wrong or very wonderfully right. So yes, you're there at every audition.

Edward Albee

We had a problem during the original Broadway production (of *Tiny Alice*), with John Gielgud playing Brother Julian. He began rehearsals by saying, "I don't understand a word of this play, not a word." And a week before we opened, we'd just started previews, I got a call that John wanted to have a meeting with the director and the producer and me. He announced that he couldn't possibly do that eleven-minute monologue—nobody could do it. And I said, "Well, John, if anybody can do it. . . ."

"Nooo," he said.

And I got rather annoyed during that meeting. I remember—I don't know how I had the nerve to do it—I said, "Well, John, there are three choices. You can either do the first half of the monologue—you know, the first five-and-a-half minutes. Or, you can start in the middle and do the second five-and-a-half minutes—stop. Or, we can do 'Hits from the Monologue.'"

There was a long silence; and then John said, "Very funny, Edward. Very funny."

Christopher Durang

I started to value some of the feedback I got from actors a little more than some of the feedback I got from other writers. Not that the writers weren't smart; but they sometimes came so much from their own point of view. An actor is usually coming from, *How can I make this piece work?* The feedback they give is just very valuable.

Arthur Kopit

What the actor does is awesome. And when they're doing something, they're giving you a gift. They become naked. They're on a tightrope and there's no safety net.

Robert Anderson

It's difficult if a director says, "I love that actor," and you think, *Oh, my God, he's terrible.* That's where you learn to get along with people. Maybe you see a slightly better actor four days later and say, "This one is better."

Paula Vogel

The directors and the actors are going to show you every flaw in the rehearsal process.

Bill Russell

When I'm directing my own work, with *Elegies*, I would often think, working with an actor, *Who wrote this? You know, this is terrible.*

Edward Albee

I learned from Beckett and Chekhov that there is a certain precision involved in playwriting, and if you really think you know the way you want a line to sound, and the intention of the whole piece, you can be very specific without limiting the actor's creativity.

Richard Easton

One always has to remember that the playwright is the artist in the theatre, and the actor is a craftsman.

6

The Director

John Tillinger

Sometimes, playwrights don't know what they've written and you have to explain it to them.

Samm-Art Williams

Producers and directors have a tendency to treat writers like kids. All of a sudden, it becomes their show. That's where the problem lies. They don't realize that this writer has created these characters out of his mind and heart and body; and nobody is going to give you that and let you do what you want.

Gregory Mosher

You have to serve the play, as an actor must serve the play, with courage and love and fortitude and brio and all of those things. But finally, you have to go back to the play—so absolutely, it's the writer's.

Robert Anderson

The director is the writer's surrogate when the play gets into the theatre. You all probably know the protocol: that the playwright does not talk to the actors, he or she talks to the actors through the director.

It's very difficult. When I teach playwriting, I say that half of the job is learning how to write a play. The other half is learning how to get along with people.

It is this delicate balance. And that's why the playwright must not talk to any of the actors since each director has worked up a separate line, a channel of communication with each actor, and some actors like to be told to get up, take three steps, and sit down. Others, before they get up, they have to tell you all about their mother or her death, or something of that sort. Others want to be taken out for a drink and have everything explained. It's a different channel. And if the playwright suddenly comes in and violates that channel, it's terrible.

Christopher Durang

I guess my preference is the director who is free and easy, and doesn't mind if you talk—particularly in rehearsal. I think if you take the actor aside privately, that's not a good thing to do. I have worked with directors who are stricter and would prefer you not. And then, I do my best to obey that.

Martin Charnin

A playwright, I assume, is the lonelier of the two, as far as directors and playwrights are concerned. I think the playwright sits there and writes it, whatever the *it* is. The director comes to the piece after something exists.

John Guare

You find the style of the play; for me, it evolves out of the very collaborative connection between the playwright and the director during the audition process.

Terrence McNally

Theatre is collaboration, and if you're not singing from the same chart, you're going to have chaos. You're going to have a twelve-tone musical, which no one wants to hear.

Brian Clark

I enjoy my work being subjected to the top creative minds from other disciplines. That doesn't mean to say in my contract I won't have director and cast approval. And I expect a director to have the same. But that only gives me an equal shot. Having got that, having got a director that I feel we can work with, and a cast that both of us approve, then we're in there pitching equally. That's the process I really enjoy. When that works, it's a marvelous experience.

Robert Aguirre-Sacasa

I definitely have an admiration for directors who can figure out how to talk to actors and designers in a way that I couldn't.

Arthur Kopit

I have worked with directors who could explain the play perfectly. Then, they got onstage and they didn't know what they were doing.

Douglas Carter Beane

It somewhat irritates me when you become a good writer, and you get to know writing, to see a play that has just been trashed. And you know the play is good. It was a lazy director. It was a bad director. And that is an anger that is a deep-seated anger. You just say, *Oh, tell her to put the damn cup down and let's hear the lines. These are beautiful lines.*

David Auburn

I've never had any major conflicts with a director. But I think this is because when you are first starting out, you make sure that you both have, essentially, the same idea of what you want for the play—that he doesn't think he's directing a farce when you've written something that's more serious. There's the basic questions of tone: What kind of production should this be? Should it be an essentially realistic production? Or, something more abstract? If you're on the same page with those things, I think, then any disagreements you have further down the line are going to be relatively minor and things that you can work through.

Lloyd Richards

August Wilson knew very little about theatre. He's a poet. So, when he came and started writing his initial plays—if you go back and look at the old scripts, or I do—there's not always a sense of place and time. A character might stay in a scene and not speak for pages and pages, and be forgotten and come back. Those are things that over the years the playwright has learned to do. So, you don't find those things in the later scripts. The working relationship alters in those respects, in terms of the knowledge.

We talk very little since we seem to understand what one another's going to say before [the other says] it. You say the things that are essential, and not the unessential things.

David Auburn

I was thinking nervously, *This is my first big show. What's going on?* And I finally came back into rehearsal of *Proof* after a week-and-a-half, and I was really anxious to sit down with Dan Sullivan and ask, "How did everything go? What's going on? How is it?" And he looked at me and said, "It's good." And that was it. And I knew it was good, and he was being very straightforward. If there had been anything that I needed to worry about then, he would have told me.

John Rando

That relationship, between the writer and the director, is a very complicated relationship, which has many different facets to it. With Neil Simon, a lot of times, by saying nothing to him you say a lot. He would call and send me a rewrite of a scene—he'd fax it from Los Angeles. And I would read it, and I'd realize it wasn't yet finished. And so, I would call and say, "Hello, Neil." And there would be a pause. And then he'd say, "OK, I'll go back to work on it." I wouldn't even say anything.

Then, he'd send it back later on—the next day, or later that day—another change, and I would read it. And I would immediately call: "Hello, Neil?" And he knew. "It's great, isn't it?"

Arthur Kopit

In Russia, because the directors have so much time and the theatre is director-driven—the writers basically don't write plays on their own, they only wait for a director to hire them to write a play.

Very often, the pieces had dazzling theatrical moments, amazing form. But what I discovered afterward, which I was sensing from watching the play without understanding it, was that there was no story going from beginning to ending. And the writers' great frustration is that they have no control whatsoever over this.

Arthur Miller

Unfortunately, I do sometimes direct something. But I think that it depends entirely on the director, and the cast, even, as to what the division of responsibility is going to be. And it depends, of course, a lot on the playwright. Some playwrights feel that they know better than anybody what ought to be up there. Other playwrights feel they know nothing about what ought to be up there and await a happy surprise.

John Tillinger

I did two revivals of Arthur Miller's plays, *After the Fall* and *The Price*, and they were both successful—up to a point. In fact, they were really quite successful. But one thing I would say about Arthur is, he's the most pragmatic man.

When I did *After the Fall*, I suggested that the part of the brother did not work. And he said, "Well, it doesn't work? Cut it." And I wish other playwrights had that attitude. He's very pragmatic in that way.

John Guare

That recklessness of the bored director can be great, remarkable—a nightmare experience.

Richard Greenberg

I worked for several years with the same couple of directors. And they're wonderful directors; and once you find a director you like, you tend to stick to him or her.

Richard Nelson

Mostly, for me, the training has been very simple. I spent twenty-some years sitting next to, close to, behind, around some of the greatest directors of the English—speaking world: people from Trevor Nunn to Liviu Ciulei to David Jones or Roger Michell or John Madden, an extraordinary group. You've got a number of people—Peter Gill—an amazing range of directors, and I learned from each and was in awe of each, and enjoyed each. And it's come a time, in my own writing, that I've learned that now what I want to see on the stage and how it works are so entwined that I feel that maybe I'm the best person, or the easiest person, to convey that, relay that, organize it.

Michael Frayn

I have to say, it's a very unfair relationship, because if the director works on a new play, nobody who sees the play knows what the writer's done and what the director's done. So, the writer usually gets the credit for it.

Timothy Mason

Directors can communicate. A good director knows how to communicate with an actor. And over the years, I've learned just to sit back and watch them work, and bite my tongue when I think they're going wrong; and even to curl up on a sofa at the back of the rehearsal room and fall asleep.

John Pielmeier

I've been in situations with a director that takes the show down a certain path, and it's a while before I realize what has been done and what's gone wrong here. And that's very scary. But I find that's a hazard of the game in a way. How could you be totally open and not be vulnerable to sideswipes?

Kia Corthron

More recently, I've had much better collaborations with directors. I've met people whom I work with well. And the interesting thing is, everybody has different ways of working with their directors. The directors that I have the best collaborations with—this is their idea, not mine—want me there every day in rehearsal, and at auditions, too. Sometimes, midway, I get a little bored myself. But it's interesting, since there are some directors who could be very threatened by that.

David Leveaux

For those of you who don't know Harold Pinter, one of the things he's famous for is being very, very rigorous and severe about the accuracy with which his text is delivered. In fact, this is simply because it's written so well, and it is true that if you deviate from it, then you can feel a quantum loss of energy.

But I do recall going into his dressing room one evening during the run (of *No Man's Land*) to give him a note since I felt that he was coming in on a particular line rather too quickly and this was causing a moment of incomprehension in the narrative for the audience. So I, of course, brought this to his attention, as the director to an actor: "No, actually, you can't do that, We really need the space there." Initially, he bridled. "Well, look—but I think we found, as we were playing it, in the audience, we found that actually we need to move it on there." And I said, "Actually, that's not really the experience of sitting out there where I am, Harold." And he said, "I mean, it just feels more comfortable to get on with it there."

I could feel that was going to be a rather tense exchange. I said, "Look, I have to tell you, not only do I think this is a pause, but I think you need a silence." And at this point, I had an inspiration, which was to pick up the script. I was hoping against hope that this was going to be borne out. I got to the moment, and indeed, he had written SILENCE.

I said, "There, you see?"

There was silence; and then, he said to everyone in the dressing room—because they were all sharing a dressing room, this was a small theatre in London—"What the director is telling me here is when the writer wrote silence he knew what he was doing. And I shall observe that."

Richard Greenberg

I have a very vague, a very abstract sense. It feels specific, but really, if I were to put it into words, what I'm seeing, it would be blue, do you know what I mean? I think it should be blue. And then, when you have a director who's keyed in and designers who are keyed in, suddenly you see what you meant by blue. But it's broken down into thousands of minor gestures.

Douglas Carter Beane

The beauty, the genius part of being a writer is that at any moment you can get up and leave the room, and nobody freaks out. I can be at the very first performance, I can get up and, *Bye-bye now.*

If I were a director and I did that, people would die. They would just fall down and die. "Look, he just left."

But also, I think you want someone there looking at it. You want to worry about the words and the images. You don't want to have to worry about Becky Sue's cup of coffee: *Where does that go?*

David Esbjornson

I love having the playwright in the room, because when the author talks and sometimes reads the play—not too often anymore—just the stories they tell, the way they speak, those are really strong indications of how the play should be.

Richard Greenberg

I like a director who never stops hectoring me. I loved it. And it was hard. It was exhausting. There were times I felt I'd come to my limit, *I can't do this anymore.* And we had fights. Not antagonistic fights. But I'm really good about cutting. I've usually been self-motivated, and I like cutting. But he wanted to take stuff out I didn't want to take out. And finally, he was always right. He was always right.

Arthur Miller

I saw Michael Blakemore's production of a play of mine called *All My Sons,* which I saw in London. And I had never seen, except in one other production in Jerusalem, a production of that play in which the central character was the mother. It threw me back to the time when I was writing the play and when indeed, before it got cast and before it got directed, and before it got acted.

Julia Jordan

I work with the director Joe Calarco. This will be our third time working together. And I just feel like I'm going to hold onto him for life. We've had that perfect relationship in which I can be really, really bad. I can write really, really bad stuff, and he has no qualms about telling me. And we're both screamers, and we don't hold it against each other. It's just perfect.

Richard Nelson

I once had a play—real big problem—where a director almost had his hands around your throat as a playwright, saying, "Cut it. Change it": in another production, no problem at all. And to learn that, learn what your center and what your place is, as opposed to going left and right, and being bounced around—it's the hardest thing.

Paula Vogel

You know you've got a good collaboration when you have really good fights.

Arthur Miller

I could go on talking about this for days. But I'll spare you everything by saying that it's simply like a marriage in effect.

You find somebody you think you can live with, and sometimes you're lucky, and that turns out to be the case. And sometimes you're not so lucky, and new sides to his or her personality begin to develop.

John Pielmeier

The ideal relationship, I think, is a marriage.

7

The Writer Directing

Richard Nelson

I always, if I'm directing my own play, on the first day I tell the actors that I'm going to do what I think every director I've ever worked with has secretly wanted to do, and that's throw the playwright out of the room.

Edward Albee

I've been directed by a lot of really good directors over the years. But something occurred to me a long time ago, which is when I write a play I see it and I hear it as I write it, as a performed piece onstage. I don't begin writing it in some kind of ephemeral reality; I see it being performed. And I keep that vision with me.

And it occurred to me that if I could learn the craft of being a director, the one thing that I could give an audience—which is not necessarily the thing they want—but the one thing I could give them is a very accurate representation of the play that I saw and heard while I was writing it.

That's why I started directing my own work.

But it never occurred to me that there was any craft involved in directing when I started out. And so, I started directing my work knowing nothing about directing. And the first play of mine I ever directed was a production of *The Zoo Story,* deep in the foothills of Pennsylvania, fortunately. Because it was, without question, the worst production of any play of mine I've ever seen.

And then it occurred to me that maybe there was some craft. That production of *The Zoo Story* made it quite clear that the director—who happened to be me, the author—had no idea what the play was about. Or, if I did have any idea what the play was about, I had absolutely no way to communicate with the actors. *So maybe,* I thought, *I should start learning the craft of being a director.*

Jonathan Tolins

I have also directed a number of shows. But I decided for myself that I preferred not to direct my own plays, for the very reason Mr. Albee likes to. I find that, if I'm directing a play of my own, I do it exactly as I pictured it. And then, I find that there's probably a lot there that can be found by somebody who doesn't have that idea going into it.

Lawrence Sacharow

The thing that was different about Edward Albee is he's extremely specific and clear about: what he writes is what he wants. In rehearsal, I remember doing certain kinds of staging and saying, "Well, now, Edward's going to say, 'Get rid of that.'" And I thought, *Well, we're going to try everything. And then, I want him to say, "Let's get rid of a couple of things."* And I knew what he would focus on, and I did it because it was interesting and it was good for the actors to do it, even though it didn't end up in the play.

And then, true enough, he came and he saw that, and he said, "All right, that is not in keeping with my play." So, we got rid of it.

Emily Mann

I'm a bit schizophrenic about it. There's one side of my brain that would love never to direct one of my plays. And there's the other side that felt impelled to, for numerous reasons.

Tony Kushner

There's a lot of prejudice about playwrights directing their own work that is not, I think, ultimately valid. Playwrights can sometimes be wonderful directors of their own work. I think it can be difficult if your work is still in progess, to be alone with it, with a cast.

And I also think that, just on a purely technical level, directing takes a great deal of time. And so does playwriting. What I'm having trouble with is figuring out how to spend enough time writing and to sort of ease myself back into directing. I think that it's hard to do both in one lifetime.

David Henry Hwang

I've directed a couple of times. I directed some of my early work, and I've directed some other plays, mostly in the Bay area, when I was younger. And I think what I basically found is that I don't mind directing. But I'm too lazy to do it. I don't really like having to show up every day. I like sitting at home and writing.

Tom Dulack

Well, I just directed a production of *Breaking Legs* in Pasadena, and the director–author relationship was perfect. I was on a panel, I think, in 1991. At that point, I said that I found, basically, directors a necessary evil. As I get older, I find them an unnecessary evil. I like to direct my own work. And flying in the face of all conventional wisdom on this matter, I think more and more playwrights are directing their own work now.

Robert Anderson

I think that most playwrights have acted at one time or another. I think that to see what the directors and actors are up against would be helpful.

I'm against it.

I've been asked and told by everybody to direct my own plays, but I've always been against it. I would be very literal. The director finds out similes, images, and so on to give to the actors.

Douglas Carter Beane

You've got to shut up and listen to other people, and work with them. And in a weird way, though you do say, *This is mine and I own it,* you have to say, *Go, and let me be there to inform you of what I was trying for; and you tell me what you're going for.*

Bill Russell

I don't necessarily like to direct my own stuff. But in the case of *Elegies,* which has the structure of *Spoon River Anthology,* it's written in free-verse monologues, interspersed with songs. When I started doing the initial readings, it was just convenient for me to direct. And as I directed, it was an incredible experience—working with actors on it. I'd ask,

That's there? I wrote that there? I found all of this stuff that I just wasn't conscious of as a writer, which was in the poems that I discovered as a director with actors.

Because it was such a personal piece and written in verse, I felt very much about my rhythms and I really enjoyed doing it. So I did continue to ask, when it was produced in London, that I direct.

And, of course, a lot of people would say, "No, that's the worst idea, an author directing his own work." But they let me get away with it.

Adam Rapp

I felt more involved when I was directing. Because I find that when I'm the playwright in the room, I'm just like this punk-rock voice that doesn't care what the audience thinks. I become a kind of chip-on-my-shoulder-type guy in the corner.

When I'm directing, it's a continuation of the authoring for me. I'm more of an audience advocate. I really want them to be involved in every moment of the story. And my play gets better. Plus, I love working with actors.

For me, I was really afraid to do it at first. But I'd always had this instinct. And I forget that I'm the playwright. I just want to make the story work. I'm not precious about my words. I'm not precious about moments that aren't working.

Brian Clark

I have tried directing my own play once. It was a small play in the Fringe in London. And I remember there was a line that I loved. I think I'd have cut the whole play and just have this line spoken. The actor hated it. Unfortunately, on one night he had to go and record a television play, so I said I would play that night instead of him. And I didn't have time to rehearse it. I learned the words, I had a quick rehearsal with the actors before I went on. And I got to this line, and it was unspeakable. I came off afterward and said to the other actors, "How did the director let the writer get away with a line like that?"

Marshall W. Mason

It's often—often, not always—a very bad idea for a playwright to direct his or her own work, because the peak of creativity really comes at two different times in the two different creative fields. The writer's peak happens in that first impulse, and then the rewrite is real hard work. But the reason it's so hard is that you're doing it without that original inspiration. The director, it is to be hoped, in the preproduction period, and with the actors during the rehearsal period, is operating at his or her peak.

Paula Vogel

I've directed my own work. And I think that there can be a tendency to correct the problems of the script directorially. Which means as long as you're directing, it's fine. But if someone who doesn't know you picks it up, they don't know what's in your mind.

8

The Dramaturg

Paula Vogel

Believe me, I'm very pro-dramaturg.

John Patrick Shanley

I have no interest in them.

Don Scardino

Dramaturgs tend to come from an academic background.

Marshall W. Mason

It's been discovered in the European theatres that there
needed to be, besides the director and the writer, someone

who was watching out for the values of the production in a social and political context—to make sure that the voice of the author was really being heard, and that there was no danger of being constantly buried under production values.

Edward Albee

There's nothing wrong with a dramaturg, I suppose, as long as it's not somebody with an agenda, or somebody who is trying to shape the politically correct aesthetic of a particular regional theatre. I think dramaturgs turn up much more in regional theatres than they do anywhere else.

As long as they're not limiting what happens in the theatre, or shaving off all the rough edges, then they're OK. It's nice to have somebody involved in the theatre who can read.

Tony Kushner

I find—at least in the regional theatres in this country, which is where I've spent most of my time working—that the danger actually comes before people get in front of an audience; that the rough edges are mostly sanded off by diligent hands that are all over the script. Dramaturgs and directors, and assistant and associate artistic directors, and people who work in the theatre, sort of making it in the process—theatre product—before it ever gets a chance to get out in front of an audience.

Marsha Norman

I think playwrights, by and large, find that they would like to be left alone. Although, clearly, dramaturgs love the theatre and know what it is.

David Ives

I actually have often dreamed of honoring dramaturgs and giving them a small coastal country and letting them talk to themselves. And then, taking a jackhammer and cutting that country off at the border and floating it out into the sea.

Ernest Schier

I don't think a literary manager is quite a dramaturg, or a dramaturg is quite a literary manager. My broadest definition, worked out simply for myself in terms of my own work at The O'Neill and at Pan Asian Repertory, is that a dramaturg is an advocate for the playwright. And sometimes, he needs to be actively that, or he's a mother, or he's an emergency-medical service.

But what I'd like to emphasize is that a dramaturg is not a play doctor. He is not concerned with writing or rewriting the playwright's work in any situation. He can be interpretive or analytical.

Erin Sanders

The dramaturg will be different on every production, depending somewhat on the needs. But the short definition I use is the theatrical equivalent of an editor on a production. You give suggestions of cuts or suggestions consisting of changes. But again, it's very clear you've not a play doctor at all. You're not there to fix something. You're there to give insight into what the playwright is trying to achieve, and if the play is achieving that goal.

Marshall W. Mason

Today, the dramaturg in America is really someone who is an expert on structure, someone who asks a question like, *What happens to this character?* It's the sort of function that Kazan really performed with Williams in the third act of *Cat on a Hot Tin Roof:* asking, "What happened to Big Daddy? He's a very important character and I feel he must come back." That's a dramaturgical question: What happens to the play? That's what the function is.

Terrence McNally

Plays with dramaturgs get sort of homogenized, I feel. I go to the theatre to hear the unique voice of a writer, not what someone has fashioned it into. They were not around when I started writing plays. Everybody had their own voice. A play by Lanford Wilson was nothing like a play by Edward Albee.

Terrence McNally

The notion of Eugene O'Neill and a dramaturg is mind-boggling. They would just have had a heart attack with one of his scripts.

Jerry Zaks

I'm just in awe of writers. As a result, I'm not a very good dramaturg.

Jonathan Tolins

I think that the whole wave of dramaturgs now seems to resemble most for me what I see in Hollywood, which is called the development process or Development Hell as everyone calls it.

The danger is that very often now playwrights will be assigned a dramaturg at a theatre and there's never any promise of a production. It isn't leading toward an actual production. It's just someone to work on the play to lead it toward how they think it should go.

You may not end up with a better play. You may end up with a play that pleases this person who has a desk job. And so I think that can be a danger.

Christopher Durang

I'm sure there were some people who were unhappy with Edith Oliver's reviews in *The New Yorker*. But I always thought that in many ways she was a very kind reviewer. I think her working as a dramaturg [at the O'Neill Theater Center] gave her a lot of insight about how hard it is to write a play.

Timothy Mason

If God had a dramaturg, would we have an armadillo? Or a horseshoe crab? There is something funny-looking that comes out of the subconscious. And if you neaten it up, you know, it's lost.

Terrence McNally

A good director, a good actor, is a good dramaturg.

9

The Place Is the Thing

André Bishop

I think the conditions to be a playwright in America—and I know everyone wants me to say they're appalling—are excellent. I think we, because of the nonprofit theatre, have been living in a golden age of American playwriting.

Edward Albee

There are very, very, very few, maybe one a year, good, serious, American plays, which are tolerated and permitted to exist on what we call Broadway. The really serious American theatre is off-Broadway, off-off-Broadway, regional theatres, and university theatres.

Becky Mode

One of my experiences with just taking our play *(Fully Committed)* from place to place is we went upstate to the Adirondacks, and people told us, "Well, it's a very New York play and people won't get it in the Adirondacks." Or in Rhinebeck. And it was a different type of audience from what we were used to. But I was prepared for an icy silence.

The thing that was nice for me was seeing how different audiences respond differently: that they did respond to it, but they responded to different things in the play. It seemed a little obnoxious that credit wasn't being given, as though New York audiences were somehow smarter and more gifted and more smug. Maybe they got different references, but it was an equally good audience. In fact, it was a great audience.

Between Broadway and off-Broadway, I don't know. But I will say that between our noncommercial and our commercial run there's a different expectation. Partly, they're just paying more, so you feel they're crankier if it's not what they thought it was going to be.

John Pielmeier

When I saw *Closer*, a play that I thought was really wonderful. It made me quite sad at the end because I thought, *If this exact play had been written by an American playwright, it would not be on Broadway at this moment. It would be off-Broadway.* Because I think, critically, it came to Broadway with the raves already written from London. The equivalent of that in America would be regional, possibly having started off-Broadway. And you can have all the regional raves in the world and it's not going to help. They're almost going to work against you critically on Broadway.

Edward Albee

If your goal is only a two-thousand-seat theatre, then maybe you'll have some problems. There are a lot of good, sympathetic theatres around this country, many of them as far away from New York as you can get.

Emily Mann

Most writers now, I think, say, "Avoid New York as long as possible. Let your play live."

Tony Kushner

What's exciting for me about a New York audience is that it is exactly that. It is, in a sense, a national audience. If you have a play running in New York, over the course of a few months, every kind of person that lives in this country will come through the theatre.

John Pielmeier

Traditionally, we're brought up in this country believing that Broadway is the end-all and be-all. And in reality, of course, as theatre professionals, we realize rather quickly it's not that at all.

John Guare

If you have a rotten experience off-Broadway, you're not going to have a great experience on Broadway. If that gets to be an issue, then it's a play that's not going to transfer.

I think that it would be within the playwright's purview to say that—if a play he had written for a ninety-nine seat theatre were suddenly going to transfer to the Broadway theatre, to the Gershwin, a two-thousand-seat theatre—"My play will die there, and you can't do it no matter what star has come in."

Tom Dulack

I got to the Long Wharf by a most extraordinary accident. John Tillinger and Arvin Brown both told me this story. We did a reading in '74 of a play that never got produced, and in '78 or so, John said that he went over to Arvin's house one night, and Arvin said, "For God's sake, do something with that pile of plays," which numbered about three-hundred at that point. "Do something. Get rid of them." And Tillinger began leafing through and he said, "There's a play by Tom Dulack in this heap." And Arvin asked, "Who's Tom Dulack?" And he said, "We did a reading by this guy a few years ago." He took the play home and read it, and by that accident . . . you know, if Arvin hadn't been housecleaning that particular night, I wouldn't be here today.

Paula Vogel

It's very interesting what plays are done off-Broadway versus what's done commercially. What is, for me, a great thing right now is that there are a lot more holes-in-the-wall with younger producers, and that there's actually a vitality out in the regional theatre as well as in the downtown theatre, of plays that run for three weeks, with plays that are done on a five-thousand-dollar budget, with plays that are being written by twenty-one-year-olds.

Tony Kushner

Even now, with as many regional theatres as there are and with a lot of them going bankrupt, I think that for Latino playwrights, African American playwrights, and women, it's still enormously difficult, even for very, very good writers to get productions.

Robert Anderson

Repertory theatre is grand for the actor, but it's not much for the playwright. I still am one of the people who, if you fight it out, want the Broadway theatre.

Geraldine Fitzgerald

Off-Broadway and off-off Broadway are the really creative theatrical media now, in my opinion. That is where new work can be created and emerge the way the playwright would like to see it.

I've found the pressure of working on Broadway was terribly difficult. I'm glad I got the chance, and I'm glad that I survived it. It's not anything that's creatively enjoyable.

Michael Price

Beyond just nurturing the writer, I think that the regional theatre, more than Broadway, has given writers and artists the right to fail.

Emily Mann

Now, the writers are saying, "Well, let's go to England first." You can do eight in the region. But if you go to London and they like it in London, then they won't dare pan you in New York.

John Pielmeier

As writers, it's important to think about where we want the play to end up. Certainly, colleges around this country are totally capable of doing plays with casts of twenty or thirty. But we never think of that in terms of regional or New York theatre—and that, obviously, because of the budget limitations of those places: they are going to limit, in effect, how we write plays.

Paula Vogel

I've never been done on Broadway. I am an off-Broadway baby. It's sort of, *I didn't find the New York apartment in time, so I ended up in Providence. If I had found that New York apartment, I'd still be a New Yorker.*

It's a similar thing in terms of how I got here, from the staged readings and the holes-in-the-wall that did me, the tiny fifty-seat theatres in Juneau, Alaska, or Theatre Rhinoceros, or Wired Woman Productions.

It is occurring to me, as I get older, that there's a glass ceiling of Broadway and that I won't go through that glass ceiling.

Jack Tantleff

I think one of the big problems is a problem in the country at large. Things have become so conservative—regional theatres are afraid to offend their subscribers in any way because all around us regional theatres are failing every single day and so, whereas [in the mid-1980s] there were a lot of theatres that were doing a lot of new plays by writers nobody had heard of, now there are a certain number of theatres

who say they are. But in fact, they need known quantities—
and they need known quantities that are writing plays that
are safe.

Lloyd Richards

There are as many different personalities as there are theatres, which means there are as many different tastes and as
many different ways of functioning. There are theatres where
you can go and mail a script in, attention will be paid, and
you will get it back in two or three weeks. There are others
that take up to four or five months.

That they take a script and read it, and get back to you
at all [is impressive]—the economics of reading plays is very
big. It costs a theatre: every play that they have read.

I imagine that most regional theatres get over two-thou-
sand plays a year.

Edward Albee

We're not terribly unhappy necessarily—well, matter of fact,
we're often quite happy to have our plays done in a five-
hundred-seat theatre, with an enthusiastic audience. It is a
kind of second-class citizenship. But that doesn't bother
us much.

10

Final Illuminations

Jonathan Tolins

I feel the writing is not the hard part. It's having something worth saying that's difficult.

Daisy Foote

I love playwrights that can tell a good yarn.

Edward Albee

I hold to the premise that any play that cannot be done with one naked light bulb and a couple of chairs probably has something slightly wrong with it.

Adam Rapp

Maybe our narrative minds are being quickened by MTV and iPods—you know, the click-and-drag culture that we are. Maybe kids these days process information so much faster. But I like to think of myself as a preservationist. And I like to think that the two-hour play, the two-and-a-half-hour play, is just as valid as it was ten years ago. If you're telling a good story, anybody would listen for four hours.

Paula Vogel

The reason that I am still in love with theatre is that it is an emotional reality. It is not surface reality. It asks us to take an emotional journey. It is not Reality TV. It is not everybody's reality. I want to go to the theatre and walk inside someone else's shoes and get inside someone else's skin, and leave my own body behind. That's why it's crucial for us in a democracy to have theatre, because it's not done by test-marketing.

Moisés Kaufman

There is a great hunger for new forms. I think that the success or resonance of the plays has been not only because of the subject matter, but also because people are saying, *Oh, I never knew the theatre could do this, or could be that way.* The question is, *What is the thing that can happen in the theatre that doesn't happen in film and television?*

Lisa Kron

A script, it seems to me, is a blueprint for this thing that happens on a stage—and then this thing that happens with an audience. It's always incomplete unless you're having that interaction with the audience.

Brian Clark

Someone once said recently, I can't remember who, "The playwright's spiritual ancestor is not a poet but a juggler."

Jack Tantleff

Most struggling writers look at the world of theatre as being kind of a brick wall, nobody wants to hear from them. In point of fact, exactly the opposite is true. There is huge hunger out there for new work, for new writers

Paula Vogel

You should submit your work to theatres that are doing the work that you love. Do that research. Submit to them. And when someone sends you a letter, lick your finger and run it over the ink. If the ink runs and an actual person signed that letter, it means that someone read your play. It wasn't rejected in the first cut. It was read by two readers, and they're encouraging you. They're not rejecting you. Write a note back to that person by name and thank him. And within five years, that person will be opening the door and mentoring to you, and helping you form your career.

John Patrick Shanley

The one thing that I've found to be true is that we're all scared to say who we are. We're all scared to tell the truth. We'll do anything rather than tell the truth. And when you do tell the truth—and by the truth, I mean what is true for you—in that moment, the audience likes it. They're interested. They're with you. They smell it.

Douglas Carter Beane

After the reviews came out for *The Little Dog Laughed*, I showed up at the theatre to get my flowers and presents the next day. And the stagehand said, "Yeah, the reviews are good." And I said, "Yeah, they really were nice. Hopefully, we'll run." He said, "You keep writing them and we'll keep loading them in."

The writer writes it and that's what happens. We're all just part of the business. We're all in it together, you know? I love that.

Regina Taylor

I hate admitting fear, but absolutely, I'm scared to death. And that is the process. I think you grow from it. You learn from it. And you say, *Well, OK, I'll live through it,* and hope someone will produce you again.

Daisy Foote

Just keep writing. I know that's really frustrating, but that's really what it is. If you want guaranteed success, don't be in this business.

Nilo Cruz

That's what I love and that's what I enjoy the most: when I'm immersed in the writing process.

Arthur Kopit

You have to have some invulnerable core that believes in what you're doing and says, *This is what I do.*

Another thing is being connected to other people who do the same thing in some way. Writers have to know other writers: having community, and respecting other artists' work. And when a fellow-writer or actor is moved by your work, or an audience that you don't know, there's the juice.

Paula Vogel

You know very talented friends that you would love to work with. Be true to each other. Be generous and believe in each other; because, it's hard to sustain one's belief alone, all isolated. Circles will rise together. If there are people you would love to work with who are in your class, in your neighborhood, be true to them and you will rise together.

John Guare

I like making a theatrical event. But if I couldn't write, I'd work in the theatre. I don't know. I've sold orange juice, I've checked coats. I'm serious; I love working in the theatre, and that's my job.

Richard Greenberg

The most exhilarated I've been has been standing in the back, a few feet away from the audience, watching my play, and having it happen to me—experiencing the event as if I didn't know what was about to happen. And feeling the others; feeling that an audience is getting what I mean.

Kia Corthron

I'm very excited by that live connection between audience and the people onstage. This is a singular moment that will never be repeated. It's this connection between those people in the audience and these people onstage—on this evening: all that immediacy is very exciting for me.

Mark Brokaw

The wonderful thing about the theatre is that the writer wins—and he has to win, because it's about language. It's about language and people. And so, the writer knows best, ultimately.

Paula Vogel

I'll bet every theatre artist will say this: there's also the search for an alternative-family structure, of a place to belong. Whether it's in Maryland or South Dakota, or wherever—when you get into that rehearsal hall, it can be in high school or it can be *Goldilocks*, you say, *I'm home now.*

Paul Rudnick

It's the exhilaration. When things go well, there's no greater high. It's just why theatre will never die, because you only get that level of ecstasy from a live audience, when the response is going well—when it shoots the actors that much higher. There's nothing like it on earth.

Theresa Rebeck

I said to some students one time, "You know, this is going to ruin your life, to be a playwright. So, make it worth it."

Richard Nelson

I love the life of a writer, there's nothing greater.

Jeanine Tesori

Basically, it starts with a blank page—and that would be us.

Arthur Miller

The theatre is just more of a personal medium. And traditionally—although this, too, is changing I'm told—the writer was the king. And he should be.

Cast of Participants

The following biographical sketches are, inevitably, far from complete. They are meant as a sampling of the work of the people excerpted in this book. These notes focus almost exclusively on stage work, consistent with the theme of the Working in the Theatre *series. Because some of those included appeared on the programs many years ago, some of their credits in this section (circa 2007) may be more recent than their appearance on* Working in the Theatre.

Roberto Aguirre-Sacasa's plays include *Dark Matters, The Velvet Sky, The Muckle Man, Say You Love Satan, Based on a Totally True Story, Rough Magic,* and *The Mystery Plays.*

Edward Albee's plays include *Who's Afraid of Virginia Woolf?* (Tony); *Seascape* (Pulitzer); *Tiny Alice; A Delicate Balance* (Pulitzer); *Three Tall Women* (Pulitzer); *The Play About the Baby; The Lady from Dubuque; All Over; The Goat, or Who Is Sylvia?* (Tony); and *Me, Myself & I.*

Robert Anderson's plays include *Tea and Sympathy, I Never Sang for My Father, You Know I Can't Hear You When the Water's Running, The Last Act Is a Solo,* and *Solitaire/Double Solitaire.*

Rob Ashford won the Tony Award for Best Choreography for *Thoroughly Modern Millie.* Other credits include *Curtains* and *The Wedding Singer,* the 2002 Roundabout revival of *The Boys from Syracuse,* and the 2005 London revival of *Guys and Dolls.*

David Auburn's plays include *Proof* (Tony), *Skyscraper,* and the one-acts *Fifth Planet, We Had a Very Good Time,* and *What Do You Believe About the Future?*

Douglas Carter Beane's plays include *As Bees in Honey Drown, The Little Dog Laughed, The Country Club, Music for a Sparkling Planet, Advice from a Caterpillar, White Lies, Devil May Care,* and *Old Money;* also, books for the musicals *The Big Time* and *Xanadu.*

Susan Birkenhead has written lyrics for the musicals *Jelly's Last Jam, What About Luv?, Fanny Hackabout Jones, The Night They Raided Minsky's,* and *Triumph of Love,* as well as additional lyrics for *High Society* and *King of Schnorrers.*

André Bishop was artistic director and literary manager of Playwrights Horizons before becoming artistic director of Lincoln Center Theater. His productions include three Pulitzer Prize–winners *The Heidi Chronicles, Directing Miss Daisy,* and *Sunday in the Park with George.*

Mark Brokaw directed Broadway revivals of *Reckless* and *The Constant Wife* as well as the original off-Broadway productions of *How I Learned to Drive, The Good Times Are Killing Me, The*

Long Christmas Ride Home, *The Dying Gaul*, *As Bees in Honey Drown*, *This Is Our Youth*, and *Avenue X*.

Charles Busch's plays include *The Tale of the Allergist's Wife*, *Pardon My Inquisition*, *Our Leading Lady*, *Shanghai Moon*, *Vampire Lesbians of Sodom*, *The Lady in Question*, *Psycho Beach Party*, *Times Square Angel*, and *Red Scare on Sunset*.

Martin Charnin wrote lyrics for *Annie* (Tony), *Annie Warbucks*, *Two by Two*, *I Remember Mama*, *The First*, and *The Hot Spot*. He directed both *Annie* musicals, as well as *The First*, and revivals of *Cafe Crown* and *The Flowering Peach*.

Michael J. Chepiga's plays include *Getting and Spending* and *A Matter of Honor*.

Brian Clark's plays include *Can You Hear Me at the Back?*, *Campion's Interview*, *Lay By*, *Hopping to Byzantium*, *In Pursuit of Eve*, *Whose Life Is It Anyway?*, *Kipling*, and *The Petition*.

Kia Corthron's plays include *Light Raise the Roof*; *Breath, Boom*; *Force Continuum*; *Splash Hatch on the E Going Down*; *Digging Eleven*; *Seeking the Genesis*; *Life by Asphyxiation*; and *Come Down Burning*.

Nilo Cruz's plays include *Anna in the Tropics* (Pulitzer), *Lorca in a Green Dress*, *Two Sisters and a Piano*, *Night Train to Bolina*, *Dancing on Her Knees*, *Hortensia and the Museum of Dreams*, and *Beauty of the Father*.

Tom Dulack's plays include *Breaking Legs*, *Solomon's Child*, *Capital Crimes*, *Bright Wings*, *Friends like These*, *Incommunicado*, and *Diminished Capacity*.

Christopher Durang's plays include *Miss Witherspoon*, *A History of the American Film*, *Sister Mary Ignatius Explains It All for You, Beyond Therapy, The Marriage of Bette and Boo, Sex and Longing, Betty's Summer Vacation*, and *Laughing Wild;* also, book and lyrics for *Adrift in Macao*

Richard Easton has appeared on Broadway in *The Coast of Utopia, Noises Off, Exit the King, Henry IV, School for Scandal,* and *The Invention of Love,* for which he received a Tony. He has been a company member at the Stratford Festival in Canada and the Royal Shakespeare Company.

Fred Ebb wrote lyrics, in partnership with composer John Kander, for the musicals *Cabaret* (Tony), *Zorba, The Happy Time, Flora the Red Menace, 70 Girls 70, Chicago, Steel Pier, The Act, Woman of the Year* (Tony), *Kiss of the Spider Woman* (Tony), and *Curtains*.

Scott Elliott is artistic director of The New Group, where his directing credits include *Hurlyburly, Aunt Dan and Lemon, Comedians,* and *Abigail's Party;* Broadway credits include *The Threepenny Opera, Barefoot in the Park, The Women,* and *Three Sisters*.

David Esbjornson is artistic director of Seattle Repertory Theatre and was artistic director of Classic Stage Company. Directing credits include the premieres of *Resurrection Blues; The Ride Down Mt. Morgan; The Goat, or Who is Sylvia?; My Old Lady*; and *Tuesdays with Morrie*.

George Faison choreographed the Broadway productions of *The Wiz* (Tony), *Don't Bother Me I Can't Cope, The Moony Shapiro Songbook,* and co-directed and co-choreographed *1600 Pennsylvania Avenue*.

Harvey Fierstein's plays include *Torch Song Trilogy* (Tony), *Spookhouse, Freaky Pussy, Flatbush Tosca, Safe Sex,* and *Forget*

Him; also, books for the musicals *La Cage aux Folles* (Tony) and *A Catered Affair.*

Geraldine Fitzgerald was an acclaimed actress who late in her career branched out into other areas, conceiving the musical *Streetsongs* and directing the Broadway production of *Mass Appeal* and *Long Day's Journey into Night* for The Public Theater.

Daisy Foote's plays include *Living with Mary, God's Pictures, Farley and Betsy, Darcy and Clara, The Hand of God, When They Speak of Rita,* and *Bhutan.*

Michael Frayn's plays include *Noises Off, Copenhagen* (Tony), *Balmoral, Here, Benefactors, Alphabetical Order, Donkey's Years, Cloud,* and *Make or Break.*

Pamela Gien wrote and performed the autobiographical play *The Syringa Tree.* As an actress, she spent four seasons with the American Repertory Theatre in Cambridge and has appeared in regional theatres across the U.S.

Keith Glover's plays include *Dancing on Moonlight* and *Coming of the Hurricane;* also, book for the musical *Thunder Knocking on the Door* and a revised book for the musical *Golden Boy.*

Richard Greenberg's plays include *Life Under Water, The Author's Voice, The Maderati, Eastern Standard, The Extra Man, Night and Her Stars, Three Days of Rain, Hurrah at Last, The Dazzle, Take Me Out* (Tony), and *The Violet Hour.*

John Guare's plays include *House of Blue Leaves, Six Degrees of Separation, Marco Polo Sings a Solo, Four Baboons Adoring the Sun, Lydie Breeze, Landscape of the Body,* and *Bosoms and Neglect;* also, books for the musicals *Two Gentlemen of Verona* (Tony) and *Sweet Smell of Success.*

Marvin Hamlisch composed the scores for the musicals *A Chorus Line* (Pulitzer and Tony), *The Goodbye Girl*, *They're Playing Our Song*, *Smile*, and *Sweet Smell of Success*.

Suheir Hammad is a poet who appeared in *Russell Simmons Presents Def Poetry Jam on Broadway*.

David Henry Hwang's plays include *Yellowface*, *M. Butterfly* (Tony), *FOB*, *The Dance and the Railroad*, *Face Value*, *Golden Child*, and *Family Devotions;* also, books for the musicals *Flower Drum Song*, *Aida*, and *Tarzan*.

David Ives's one-acts have been collected and performed as *All in the Timing*, *Mere Mortals*, and *Lives of the Saints;* full-length plays include *Polish Joke* and *Don Juan in Chicago*. Also: translations of Yasmina Reza's *A Spanish Play*; adapted books of eighteen musicals for City Center's Encores!

Julia Jordan's plays include *St. Scarlet*, *Summer of the Swans*, *Dark Yellow*, *Nightswim*, *Tatjana in Color*, and *Boy*. Also: books for the musicals *The Mice*, presented as part of Harold Prince's *3hree*, and *Sarah, Plain and Tall*.

John Kander composed scores, in partnership with lyricist Fred Ebb, for the musicals *Cabaret* (Tony), *Zorba*, *The Happy Time*, *Flora the Red Menace*, *70 Girls 70*, *Chicago*, *Steel Pier*, *The Act*, *Woman of the Year* (Tony), *Kiss of the Spider Woman* (Tony), and *Curtains*.

Moisés Kaufman wrote and directed *Gross Indecency* and, with his Tectonic Theater Project, created and directed *The Laramie Project* and *33 Variations*. He directed the original production of *I Am My Own Wife*, as well as *In the Winter of Cities*, *The Nest*, and *Marlowe's Eye*.

Arthur Kopit's plays include *Oh Dad, Poor Dad, Mama's Hung You in the Closet and I'm Feelin' So Sad*; *Indians*; *Wings*; *Chamber Music*; and *The Road to Nirvana*. Also: books of the musical *Nine* and *Phantom*.

Greg Kotis's plays include *Pig Farm* and *Jobey and Katherine*. Wrote the book and co-wrote the lyrics for the musical *Urinetown*. As a member of the troupe Cardiff-Giant, co-authored six plays including *LBJFKKK* and *Love Me*.

Lisa Kron's plays include *Well* and the solo piece *2.5 Minute Ride*. Kron is a founding member of the theatre company The Five Lesbian Brothers.

Tony Kushner's plays include *Angels in America: A Gay Fantasia on National Themes* (Pulitzer and Tony); *A Bright Room Called Day; Slavs!;* and *Homebody/Kabul*. Adaptations include *A Dybbuk* and *The Illusion*. Also: book and lyrics for the musical *Caroline, or Change*.

David Leveaux's New York directing credits include *Cyrano de Bergerac, The Glass Menagerie, Jumpers, Fiddler on the Roof, Nine, Betrayal, The Real Thing, Electra, Anna Christie,* and *A Moon for the Misbegotten*.

Terrence McNally's plays include *The Ritz; Love! Valour! Compassion!* (Tony); *The Lisbon Traviata; Master Class* (Tony); *Lips Together, Teeth Apart; Deuce*; and *Dedication*. Also: books of the musicals *Kiss of the Spider Woman* (Tony), *The Rink, The Full Monty;* and *Ragtime* (Tony).

Emily Mann's plays include *Greensboro (A Requiem); Still Life; Annulla, An Autobiography; Having Our Say; Execution of Justice;* and *Mrs. Packard*. Also: artistic director of the McCarter Theater in Princeton.

Jeff Marx won the Tony Award, with his writing partner Robert Lopez, for the music and lyrics of *Avenue Q,* which they also conceived.

Marshall W. Mason was artistic director of New York's Circle Repertory Company, where he notably directed the premieres of the majority of Lanford Wilson's plays. His directing credits also include *As Is, Knock Knock,* and *Passion.*

Timothy Mason's plays include *The Fiery Furnace, In a Northern Landscape, Babylon Gardens,* and *Ascension Day.* Also: book and lyrics for the musical *How the Grinch Stole Christmas.*

Eve Merriam created the long-running off-Broadway musical *The Club,* and wrote lyrics for *Inner City,* based on her book *The Inner City Mother Goose.*

Arthur Miller's plays include *All My Sons* (Tony), *Death of a Salesman* (Pulitzer and Tony), *The Crucible* (Tony), *A View from the Bridge, After the Fall, The Price, The Archbishop's Ceiling, The American Clock, Broken Glass, The Ride Down Mount Morgan, Resurrection Blues,* and *Finishing the Picture.*

Becky Mode is the author of *Fully Committed.*

Gregory Mosher is director of the Columbia University Arts Initiative. A Tony–nominated director for David Mamet's plays *Glengarry Glen Ross* and *Speed-the-Plow,* he has been artistic director of Chicago's Goodman Theatre and Lincoln Center Theater in New York.

Richard Nelson's plays include *Some Americans Abroad, Between East and West, Franny's Way, Frank's Home, Principia Scriptoriae, Madame Melville, The Vienna Notes,* and *Two Shakespearean Actors.* Also: adapted and directed *The Dead* and wrote the book for *Chess.*

Marsha Norman's plays include *'night, Mother* (Pulitzer), *Getting Out, Traveler in the Dark, Sarah and Abraham, Trudy Blue,* and *Last Dance;* also, books for the musicals *The Color Purple* and *The Secret Garden* (Tony).

Peter Parnell's plays include *The Cider House Rules,* adapted from John Irving's novel; *An Imaginary Life, Romance Language, Flaubert's Latest, Sorrows of Stephen, Hyde in Hollywood,* and *The Rise and Rise of Daniel Rocket.*

John Pielmeier's plays include *Agnes of God, Jass, Sleight of Hand, The Boys of Winter, Willi,* and *Courage;* also, the book for the musical *Young Rube.*

Michael Price has been executive producer of Connecticut's Goodspeed Musicals since 1968. Under his leadership, the company has rediscovered many classic musicals, and produced the premieres of *Shenandoah* and *Annie.*

John Rando directed the Broadway productions of *Urinetown* (Tony), *The Dinner Party, A Thousand Clowns,* and *The Wedding Singer.* His off-Broadway credits include *Mere Mortals, Polish Joke,* and *Pig Farm,* and the Encores! productions of *Strike up the Band* and *Do Re Mi.*

Adam Rapp's plays include *American Sligo, Bingo with the Indians, Blackbird, Faster, Finer Noble Gases, Gompers, Mistral, Netherbones, Nocturne, Should've Never, Stone Cold Dead Serious, Train Story, Trueblinka, Red Light Winter,* and *Essential Self-defense.*

Theresa Rebeck's plays include *Mauritius, The Scene, The Water's Edge, Bad Dates, The Butterfly Collection, Omnium Gatherum* (co-written with Alexandra Gersten-Vassilaros), *Abstract Expression, View of the Dome,* and *Sunday on the Rocks.*

Lloyd Richards founded the National Playwrights Conference at The O'Neill Theater Center, and was dean of the Yale School of Drama from 1980 to 1990. He directed the original production of *A Raisin in the Sun*, as well as the Broadway premieres of August Wilson's first six plays.

Mary Rodgers composed the musicals *Once Upon a Mattress* and *Hot Spot*, and composed songs heard in *From A to Z, Working, The Madwoman of Central Park West*, and *The Mad Show*.

Paul Rudnick's plays include *Jeffrey; I Hate Hamlet; Valhalla; The Most Fabulous Story Ever Told; The Naked Eye;* and *Mr. Charles, Currently of Palm Beach*.

Bill Russell wrote the books and lyrics for the musicals *Side Show, Pageant*, and *Elegies for Angels, Punks and Raging Queens*.

Lawrence Sacharow founded and was artistic director of River Arts Rep in Woodstock, New York. His directing credits included *Three Tall Women, Beckett/Albee*, and *The Concept*, as well as the American premieres of *Hunting Cockroaches* and *Viva Detroit*.

Erin Sanders is the coauthor of *Sally Marr . . . and Her Escorts*, and was the literary manager and dramaturg for the Second Stage Theatre.

Don Scardino was artistic director of Playwrights Horizons from 1991 to 1996, where he directed *Later Life, On the Bum, An Imaginary Life*, and *A Cheever Evening*. He directed the Broadway productions of *A Few Good Men* and *Lennon*.

Ernest Schier was a founder and the director of the National Critics' Institute at The Eugene O'Neill Theater Center. He was the longtime drama critic of *The Philadelphia Bulletin*.

Don Schlitz is the composer and lyricist of *The Adventures of Tom Sawyer*. He won a Grammy for the song "The Gambler," and his songs have been recorded by Randy Travis, the Judds, Reba McEntire, Vince Gill, Garth Brooks, Allison Kraus, and many other singers.

John Patrick Shanley's plays include *Danny and the Deep Blue Sea, Savage in Limbo, The Dreamer Examines His Pillow, Italian American Reconciliation, Four Dogs and a Bone, Psychopathia Sexualis, Cellini, Where's My Money?, Dirty Story, Doubt,* and *Defiance.*

Nicky Silver's plays include *Pterodactyls, Raised in Captivity, The Food Chain, The Altruists, The Eros Trilogy, Fat Men in Skirts, Fit to Be Tied, The Maiden's Prayer, My Beautiful Child, My Marriage to Ernest Borgnine,* and *The Agony and the Agony.*

Diana Son's plays include *Stop Kiss, Satellites, BOY, Fishes,* and *R.A.W. ('cause I'm a Woman).*

Joseph Stein wrote the books for the musicals *Fiddler on the Roof* (Tony), *Zorba, Rags. The Baker's Wife, Juno, Carmelina, The King of Hearts, So Long 174th Street, Take Me Along, Mr. Wonderful,* and *Plain and Fancy;* also, the play *Enter Laughing.*

Charles Strouse composed the musicals *Bye Bye Birdie* (Tony), *Applause* (Tony), *Annie* (Tony), *All American, It's a Bird . . . It's a Plane . . . It's Superman, Golden Boy, Annie Warbucks, Rags, Nick and Nora, Dance a Little Closer, Bring Back Birdie,* and *Charlie and Algernon.*

Jack Tantleff became co-head of the theatre department at the William Morris Agency in 2003. Representing authors, composers, and lyricists, he founded The Tantleff Office in 1986, later joining Abrams Artists Agency in 2001 when that company acquired the firm.

Regina Taylor's plays include *Drowning Crow, Crowns, The Ties that Bind, Oo-Bla-Dee, Urban Zulu Mambo, Escape from Paradise, Watermelon Rinds, Inside the Belly of the Beast, A Night in Tunisia, Mudtracks, Between the Lines,* and *Behind Every Good Man.*

Julie Taymor won Tonys for her direction and costume design of *The Lion King.* Her directing credits include *Juan Darién, The Green Bird, Titus Andronicus, The Tempest, The Transposed Heads,* and *The Taming of the Shrew.*

Jeanine Tesori composed the scores for *Violet; Caroline, or Change; Thoroughly Modern Millie* (Tony); and Nicholas Hytner's production of *Twelfth Night.*

John Tillinger's directing credits include *Another Country, A Perfect Ganesh, House* and *Garden, Loot, It's Only a Play, Breaking Legs, Getting and Spending, Absurd Person Singular,* and *Sylvia.* He was literary manager of Long Wharf Theatre in the 1970s and 1980s.

Jonathan Tolins's plays include *The Twilight of the Golds, If Memory Serves, The Last Sunday in June, The Climate, The Unveiling,* and the one-acts *Stewart's Line, The Midwife,* and *The Man that Got Away.*

Alfred Uhry's plays include *Driving Miss Daisy* (Pulitzer), *The Last Night of Ballyhoo* (Tony), *Without Walls,* and *Edgardo Mine.* Also: books for the musicals *The Robber Bridegroom, Parade* (Tony), and *LoveMusik.*

Paula Vogel's plays include *The Baltimore Waltz, How I Learned to Drive* (Pulitzer), *The Mineola Twins, Hot N Throb-*

bing, *The Long Christmas Ride Home*, *Desdemona*, *And Baby Makes Seven,* and *The Oldest Profession*.

Wendy Wasserstein's plays include *Uncommon Women and Others*, *Isn't It Romantic*, *The Heidi Chronicles* (Pulitzer and Tony), *The Sisters Rosensweig*, *An American Daughter*, *Old Money* and *Third;* also, the musical *Miami* with Christopher Durang.

John Weidman wrote the books for *Pacific Overtures*, *Assassins,* and *Big,* as well as co-wrote a revised book for *Anything Goes,* and co-created *Contact,* which won the Tony Award for Best Musical.

Samm-Art Williams's plays include *Home, Welcome Back to Black River, The Waiting Room, The Sixteenth Round, A Love Play, The Coming, The Dance on Widows' Row,* and *Brass Birds Don't Sing*.

August Wilson's plays includes *Ma Rainey's Black Bottom, Fences* (Tony and Pulitzer), *Joe Turner's Come and Gone, The Piano Lesson* (Pulitzer), *Seven Guitars, Two Trains Running, Jitney, King Hedley II, Gem of the Ocean,* and *Radio Golf*.

Lanford Wilson's plays include *The Rimers of Eldritch, Balm in Gilead, The Hot L Baltimore, Lemon Sky, Serenading Louie, Talley's Folley* (Pulitzer), *The Fifth of July, Angels Fall, Talley and Son, Burn This, Redwood Curtain, Book of Days,* and *Rain Dance*.

Jerry Zaks has directed many Broadway and off-Broadway plays and musicals, including *The Marriage of Bette and Boo, The House of Blue Leaves* (1985), *Anything Goes* (1987), *Six Degrees of Separation, Assassins, Guys and Dolls* (1992), *Smokey Joe's Cafe,* and *La Cage aux Folles* (2004).

Index of Names and Titles

Italicized pages reference the quoted speaker.

On the American Theatre Wing and CUNY TV

Dedicated to promoting excellence and education in theatre, the American Theatre Wing has been intertwined with American theatrical life for the better part of the last three-quarters of a century.

Creating opportunities for students, general audiences, and even those working in the field to expand their knowledge of theatre, ATW is best known for creating the premier award for artists working on Broadway, the Antoinette Perry "Tony"® Awards. Given annually since 1947, the Tonys have evolved from a private dinner for those in the industry into a gala celebration of Broadway that is seen across America and around the world. Presented in partnership with the League of American Theatres and Producers since 1967, and broadcast annually on CBS since 1978, the Tony Awards are at once the highest recognition of achievement on Broadway and a national event that celebrates the vitality of live theatre.

Yet, the Tonys are but one of ATW's long-running programs. For nearly fifty years, ATW has made a practice of providing support to New York City not-for-profit theatre companies, as well as to students at select New York theatre schools, including secondary, college, and graduate levels through its Grants and Scholarship Program. Each year, ATW makes grants in aggregate up to fifteen percent of the organization's budget, and over the lifetime of the program ATW has distributed almost $3 million in support.

In keeping with its mission of recognizing excellence, ATW sponsors the Henry Hewes Design Awards, acknowledging achievement in design from off- and off-off Broadway, as well as on Broadway, for designs originating in the United States. Conceived in 1965, these annual awards were originally called the Maharam Awards and later known as the American Theatre Wing Design Awards, but throughout their four decades they have cast a spotlight on all aspects of theatrical design.

The *Working in the Theatre* programs, which form the basis for this book (see the opening page), have captured more than four-hundred-and-fifty hours of oral history and insight on theatre, as the longest-running theatrical discussion series of its kind, offering sustained conversation between theatre artists.

Complementing these long-running programs, ATW has expanded into several new initiatives to broaden its reach. The year 2004 saw the debut of *Downstage Center,* a weekly theatrical interview show, produced in partnership with XM Satellite Radio. These in-depth interviews chronicle not only the current work of theatre artists, but their entire careers, in lively, free-ranging conversations.

In 2005, ATW introduced the Theatre Intern Group, a professional and social networking association of interns working on both commercial and not-for-profit theatre offices across New York City. Monthly meetings feature panels of experts exploring the opportunities available to young people entering the field, even as the meetings serve to build professional connections that will sustain the members as they advance in their careers.

The same year marked the debut of SpringboardNYC, a two-week boot camp of theatrical immersion, designed for college students and recent graduates aspiring to careers as performers. Over the course of the session, activities range from sessions on audition technique and finding an agent, to talks with prominent professionals, to advice on the financial aspects of working in the theatre and living in New York.

The American Theatre Wing maintains an archive of its media work on its Web site *www.americantheatrewing.org* where its media programs are available for free. This continually growing resource features more than four-hundred hours of audio and visual material that cannot be found anywhere else.

The current activities of the American Theatre Wing are part of a continuum of the Wing's service to the field dating back more than sixty years, when ATW was founded as part of the home-front effort to support, first, the British troops and later U.S. soldiers fighting in World War II. ATW captured the public imagination in the early years by creating the Stage Door Canteens, clubs for servicemen staffed by volunteers from the entertainment community, which grew and blossomed into branches across the U.S. and in Europe, in addition to a major motion picture and weekly radio program. When the war ended, ATW turned its attention to returning GIs by creating the American Theatre Wing Professional Theatre School, which for twenty years was a cornerstone in theatrical training. It boasted graduates such as Tony Bennett and James Earl Jones. At the same time, ATW brought theatre into hospitals and mental-healthcare facilities, as both entertainment and therapy.

From its wartime roots to its ongoing efforts to support theatre across the country, the American Theatre Wing continues to evolve in order to serve the needs of all who love theatre, whether they are students, ticket buyers, or those who create the work we all treasure.

CUNY TV, the noncommercial cable television station of The City University of New York, is the largest university television station in the United States. CUNY TV's arts, educational, and public-affairs programming reflects the commitment of the university to lifelong learning for all New Yorkers. Original programs are developed through partnerships with the city's leading cultural, civic, and business communities, as well as with international cultural institutes and consulates. CUNY TV reaches approximately 1.9 million households in the five boroughs of New York on cable channel 75, and each week about one million people watch the station. Several CUNY TV series have reached national audiences through American Public Television satellite distribution to PBS stations. CUNY TV has received five New York Emmy nominations and one Emmy Award since 2002.

This book is drawn from discussions that have taken place in the American Theatre Wing *Working in the Theatre* programs, a fixture in the New York City theatre community for more than three decades. A unique opportunity for theatre artists to engage in sustained conversations about the field, the seminars were begun in the early 1970s by ATW president Isabelle Stevenson, as panel discussions taking place at theatres around the city, pioneering the idea of allowing audiences to hear directly from artists and administrators about the creation of theatre. Since 1979, ATW has partnered with CUNY TV, the television arm of The City University of New York, to bring these discussions into homes throughout New York City; and beginning in 2003, the programs have been available to audiences internationally on the Internet, via both the ATW and CUNY TV Web sites.

The seminars on which this book is based were hosted or moderated by Theodore S. Chapin, Thomas Cott, Jean Dalrymple, Dasha Epstein, Brendan Gill, Sondra Gilman, Martin Gottfried, Mel Gussow, James Houghton, Jeffrey Eric Jenkins, Doug Leeds, Pia Lindström, Lloyd Richards, Howard Sherman, Isabelle Stevenson, Peter Stone, Wendy Wasserstein, and George C. White.

Also from Continuum in the *Working in the Theatre* series are *Acting* and *Producing and the Theatre Business*. A fourth volume, on Directing, is planned.